Paul Claudel and Saint-John Perse

Paul Claudel
and Saint-John Perse

PARALLELS AND CONTRASTS

by Ruth N. Horry

The University of North Carolina Press
Chapel Hill

Excerpts from the following works are reprinted by per-
mission of Princeton University Press: *Exile*, by St.-John
Perse, trans. Denis Devlin, Bollingen Series XV (copyright
© 1949 by Bollingen Foundation); *Eloges*, by St.-John
Perse, trans. Louise Varèse (© 1956 Bollingen Founda-
tion), Bollingen Series LV; *Winds*, by St.-John Perse,
trans. Hugh Chisholm, Bollingen Series XXXIV (© 1953
Bollingen Foundation); *Chronique*, by St.-John Perse,
trans. Robert Fitzgerald, Bollingen Series LXIX (© 1961
Bollingen Foundation); *Seamarks*, by St.-John Perse, trans.
Wallace Fowlie, Bollingen Series LXVII (© 1958 Bol-
lingen Foundation): Princeton University Press: 152 lines
of poetry to be quoted from these books. *Two Addresses*,
by St.-John Perse: *On Poetry*, trans. W. H. Auden, Bol-
lingen Series LXXXVI (copyright © 1961 & 1966 Bol-
lingen Foundation), Princeton University Press: quotes
from pp. 9, 10, 11. *The Collected Works of Paul Valéry*,
ed. Jackson Mathews, Bollingen Series XLV, volume 7,
The Art of Poetry, trans. Denise Folliot (copyright ©
1958 by Bollingen Foundation): short quote from p. 79.

In memory of my late parents, the Reverend
Albert F. B. Horry and Sarah Woodbury Horry;
and in appreciation to my sisters and brothers,
Sarah, Evelyn, Albert, and Joseph

Acknowledgments

The writer's interest in the work of Paul Claudel is one of long standing. Enthusiasm for the poetry of Saint-John Perse developed in recent years. As a Fellow in the 1964–1965 Cooperative Program in the Humanities of Duke University and The University of North Carolina at Chapel Hill (funded by the Ford Foundation), I was able to begin a comparative study of these two poets whose thought encompasses and transcends the mundane and the material. They seem to have a message for the troubled decades of the twentieth century.

I am especially grateful for the invaluable counsel of Dr. Wallace Fowlie, James B. Duke Professor of Romance Languages at Duke University. Also, I am appreciative to the Faculty Research Committee of North Carolina Central University for having granted funds for the typing of the manuscript. I wish further to express my thanks to those persons who gave encouragement and support during the period of research.

September, 1969

Contents

Paul Claudel and Saint-John Perse

I. Introduction

T. S. Eliot, in a rather succinct statement of the poet's reaction to experience, summarized a generally accepted concept in "The Metaphysical Poets": "When a poet's mind is perfectly equipped for its work, it is constantly amalgamating disparate experience. . . ."[1] Although two individuals may lead almost parallel lives, engage in similar activities, and follow almost identical careers, their experiences and reactions to these experiences can be worlds apart. This is true simply because they are two distinct human beings.

By the breadth of their poetic vision, their intuitive and metaphysical concept of reality, their view of the interrelationships of the universe, their evaluation of the poet's function as re-creator of the cosmos, and their non-traditional poetic form, Paul Claudel and Saint-John Perse are twin phenomena of the literary world of the twentieth century. This study is concerned with these two personalities who have created epic visions of the universe, Claudel's being divine in orientation, while Perse

1. *Selected Essays*, new ed. (New York, 1964), p. 247.

limits his point of view to the physical world and man's role in it.

The outer experiences of both of these writers have been world-wide, multi-faceted, and complex. By the evidence of their expressed thought, their inner world has been turbulent, perplexed, and visionary. In many instances, their works have revealed an affinity of purpose and design, yet there are striking divergences in outlook. This study proposes to present specific evidence of this affinity and to underline the points of divergence. The manner in which these two poets have amalgamated "disparate experience," expressed their view of the universe in similar and dissimilar fashion, and their conclusions as to the meaning of the human adventure constitute the scope of this study.

It is impossible to know every influence which causes an individual to become a creative artist. Almost always, however, his creative effort stems from confusion and uncertainty when confronted by the unknown and unknowable elements of the universe and man's place and destiny in it. When by some insight or intuition coupled with the forces of experience the creative urge is stimulated, then the artist is born. Claudel and Perse were victims of inner tensions of being and destiny created by personal experiences, made more acute by their passion to know and understand. Their genius and erudition made possible the expression in unique form of their ideas about the universe.

Both poets polarized their thinking on major concepts of the concrete and the spiritual. They were aware of the material world in all of its aspects; they endeavored to become aware of the essence of the spiritual. For Perse, this essence was the "Souffle Originel," the "toute-présence"; for Claudel, without ambiguity or equivocation, this essence was divine grace. And herein lies the divergence in vision. Perse regards the created world as an end in itself; Claudel views it as a continuous manifestation of divine will. The task of Claudel was perhaps more complex because his effort was to unify the material and the spiritual and to relate the dependence of the finite upon the infinite. In this, he is concerned with causal relationships, the symbolic meaning of the real and visible, the why and purpose of suffering and sacrifice, and the rapport and conflict between God's will and man's liberty. Dominating and encircling all of these concepts is man's salvation and its attainment. The didactic and homiletic character of Claudel's poetry is in direct contrast with that of Perse. Perse's consciousness of the outside world is expressed in evocative, laudatory, and classificatory form. His poetry informs but makes no effort to persuade or teach. Both poets seek to communicate to mankind their conceptualization of the visible world and man's destiny in the universe.

The symbolism of Claudel is spiiritual, dealing as it does with metaphysical concepts, yet it is grounded in the concrete. His perception of the real is total, facilitated as completely as possible by all of his faculties, innate and acquired—sight, sound, touch, taste, smell, memory, reason, imagination, knowledge. Thus Claudel has access to the multiple and varied aspects of creation, which in Thomist fashion he defines, distinguishes, and makes deductions about. In the first part of the process, Claudel follows syllogistic logic which attributes and affirms the quality of the property of the object, thus defining or naming it. The naming of it distinguishes it from all others. Claudel stipulates that a thing can only be defined and can only exist through the traits which makes it different from all others. The qualities and form which define and distinguish result from external forces and outside influences. The distinction conferred by the naming of a thing brings it into being and leads to knowledge and intelligence about it. An image constituted by a combination of sensations enables one to visualize and know an object. By assigning a word to this object, Claudel becomes master of the object thus represented, assimilates its sense, and makes it the subject of intelligence. Knowledge creates and is generated from within; intelligence is evaluative and is derived from the created thing (*Art Poétique*, 177–81).[2]

Claudel intuits spiritual meanings beneath the appearance of the real, the created thing. All of his intuitions are focused on God or God-centered. Man, endowed with spirit, is through his

2. Paul Claudel, *Oeuvre Poétique* (Paris, 1957). All references to *Art Poétique* in the text are from this edition.

senses, aware of the creative act of God and bears witness thereto. He is the coordinator, the evaluator, and he establishes the relationships of visible phenomena: "Par rapport au monde, il est chargé du rôle d'origine, de 'faire' le principe selon quoi tout vient s'ordonner . . . il est général, il est le sceau de l'authenticité. Par rapport à Dieu, il est le délégué aux relations extérieures, le *représentant* et le fondé de pouvoirs."[3] In the symbolic interpretation of phenomena, Claudel begins with the premise that each thing or being in creation is a partial image of God. He, as poet, by involving himself with the world of matter was reaching toward God. With Baudelaire, he could sense spiritual reality in the evidence of the concrete. This reality he could release because of his poetic genius, through metaphor.

According to Claude Vigée, Saint-John Perse rejects European symbolism, that of Baudelaire, Mallarmé and Valéry, in order to trace a new direction for Western poetry.[4] His mode of apperception of the world is certainly the same as Claudel's without the Thomist approach of naming, defining, and distinguishing. Perse is preoccupied with cosmic forces, the violent aspects of the elements, space, time, duration, humanity's presence and history, and universal disorder. As witness and observer of the material world, his quest is for the why and the "puissance." Never does he recognize God in the Claudelian sense as the First Cause. Even as Claudel attempted to persuade him personally by Thomist dialectics of God's existence, Perse at thirteen years of age was more persuaded of a "puissance" by a raging storm, claps of thunder, and flashes of lightning.[5] Claudel's effort to persuade almost alienated Perse in later years. Christian Murciaux writes: "Le prosélytisme de Claudel faillit faire sombrer cette amitié; Saint-John Perse . . . fut bouleversé jusqu'à en pleurer par l'éloquence impérieuse de Claudel. Mais il ne fut pas converti pour autant par cet homme 'trop cruel'."[6] The world of force became the subject of Perse's meditation, and his poetic creation is the effort to fix the relationship and

3. Ibid., p. 184.
4. *Révolte et louanges* (Paris, 1962), p. 218.
5. Ibid., p. 199.
6. *Saint-John Perse* (Paris, 1960), pp. 56–57.

establish an analogy between the cosmos and man's journey in time. Moreover, Perse synthesizes poetry and the cosmos to create reality. In his acceptance speech of the Nobel prize in literature, he said: "Car si la poésie n'est pas, comme on l'a dit, 'le réel absolu,' elle en est bien la plus proche convoitise et la plus proche appréhension, à cette limite extrême de complicité où le réel dans le poème semble s'informer lui-même."[7]

Both poets make use of a synthesized method and present a synthetic view in their artistic creation. The components of the synthesis and the dimensions of their re-creation are considered. The *Cinq Grandes Odes* of Claudel, and Perse's *Vents* and *Amers* provide some of the answers.

7. Saint-John Perse, *On Poetry*, trans. W. H. Auden, with the French text *Poésie*, Bollingen Series (New York, 1961), pp. 14–15. All references to *Poésie* in the text are from this edition.

II. The Making of the Poet

Although the orientation of this study is neither biographical nor psychological, some attention must be paid to the mold which produced the artist and the setting which shaped his personality. A different set of circumstances and another time in history obviously would have formed another individual.

Both poets found themselves in a milieu consisting of a large family: parents, other children, and older generations on the maternal and paternal sides. The presence of the latter group provided a living link with the past and a sense of family and even pride. Claudel, whose heritage reached back to Louis d'Orléans, brother of Charles VI, was born in Villeneuve-sur-Fère-en-Tardenois in Champagne. Alexis Saint-Léger Léger, who assumed the name Saint-John Perse in 1924, was born in Guadeloupe. He descended from an old French family of magistrates and landowners whose roots were in Bourgogne. Though proud of his noble heritage, Claudel readily admits that a few of his ancestors were from the *roturier* class. To this double heritage some have ascribed his fierce pride, his irascible disposition, and the internal conflicts of his early years. The attitude of Perse to his heritage was one of inordinate pride. Perhaps this is why Frizeau considered his as "un esprit très noble et grand" and rather haughty. The heritage of the blood in conjunction with the tales of the elders inevitably form a point of view and a general attitude toward the world. Another circumstance, which probably has some importance and can only be explained by a psychologist, is that Claudel was the youngest child in his family and Perse the only boy among five children. At least it may be observed that each had a certain distinction within the family. Each was alone in a certain sense, yet the object of attention. At eight years of age in his native Guadeloupe, Perse received his first horse, his first boat, and his first telescope.[1] His cosmic exploration had officially begun on land, on the sea, and in space. During these years, he was introduced to the flora and fauna of his native environment by the botanist Duss. He was also in daily contact with the people and culture of different races.

Before they were fourteen, their families had moved around in a limited sphere and finally into a radically different world, Perse's to France and Claudel's to Paris. In Paris, Claudel felt and was completely out of his native element. Never gregarious, he found it extremely difficult to adapt himself to his surroundings. In retrospect he reminisced: "O les longues rues amères autrefois et le temps où j'étais seul et un!"[2] Perse, uprooted from his childhood paradise, experienced his first sensation of exile and alienation which would continue because of his personal choices and the forces of history. The ambitions of Claudel's father for his children initiated in this youngest child from the provinces a sense of bewilderment, malaise, aloneness, and separation. In the *Mémoires Improvisés*, Claudel recalled that "la cause en grande partie de mon dépaysement était l'ennui matériel qui a accompagné mon transfert d'une petite ville de province où je me trouvais en somme en parfait bonheur avec ma famille, à Paris, où l'ambiance était complètement différente. J'ai eu à m'y

1. Jacques Charpier, *Saint-John Perse* (Paris, 1962), p. 28.
2. "Magnificat," *Oeuvre Poétique* (Paris, 1957), p. 248. All references from the *Cinq Grandes Odes* are taken from the above edition; the Ode is indicated by roman numerals and the page by arabic numerals.

adapter, et cette adaptation, qui n'a jamais été complète, a été très douloureuse."[3] The moral suffering of Claudel was especially marked at this period of his adolescence. The absence of his father, domestic strife, the impersonal relationship between teachers and students, the lack of a counselor, the effort to excel in school, the memory and fear of death, the bewildering aspects of city life, the spiritual void, all contributed to his feeling of being anchorless, and ultimately led to his serious concern about the meaning of life and the destiny of man.

Before they were eighteen, both writers had expressed the agitations of their inner drama. Claudel wrote "Endormie" between 1882 and 1883. Despite its elements of buffoonery, this play presents a central theme of the position of the poet in the world and his relationships with the world. Henri Mondor sees in this play an expression of the nostalgia of Claudel the newcomer to Paris: "La hantise nostalgique du village natal, chez ce récent déraciné si mécontent de Paris, devait être particulièrement agissante, presque obsédante, car nulle part, dans l'oeuvre ultérieure, même dans *La Jeune Fille Violaine*, n'interviendra, avec autant de prolixité, d'exubérance, l'expérience de la vie agricole. . . ."[4] Although this play was never really admired by Claudel, it is indicative of the lyrical propensities of the poet. The imagery and symbolism of woman and the sea, which recur throughout his later works, are already sketched in, though not with the insight and depth of his more mature years.

Separation, malaise, "la hantise nostalgique du village natal," these too are the sentiments of Perse in *Images à Crusoé* written when he was only seventeen years old, and published under the title *Eloges* along with *Pour fêter une enfance* and other poems in 1909. The poem "Cloches" of *Images* expresses a nostalgia for Guadeloupe:

> Ô Dépouillé!
> Tu pleurais de songer aux brisants sous la lune; aux sifflements de rives plus lointaines; aux musiques étranges qui naissent et s'assourdissent sous l'aile close de la nuit,

3. *Mémoires Improvisés,* compiled by Jean Amrouche (Paris, 1954), p. 24.
4. *Claudel plus intime* (Paris, 1960), p. 37.

pareilles aux cercles enchaînés que sont les ondes d'une con-
que, à l'amplification de clameurs sous la mer . . . (I, 63)[5]

There is a more poignant note sounded in *Pour fêter une
enfance*:

> Je me souviens des
> pleurs
> d'un jour trop beau dans trop d'effroi, dans trop d'effroi!
> . . . du ciel blanc, ô silence! qui flamba comme un regard de
> fièvre . . . Je pleure, comme je
> pleure, au creux de vieilles douces mains . . .
>
> Oh! c'est un pur sanglot, qui ne veut être secouru, oh!
> ce n'est que cela, et qui déjà berce mon front comme une
> grosse étoile du matin. (I, 23)

Frizeau, writing to Claudel in 1907, noted Perse's malaise after
the death of his father:

You know about the great misfortune which has befallen young
Léger. The poor child, in this sudden death of his father, has shown
great courage. His intelligence is keen, but he restrains himself with
a certain stoicism, a fear of revealing himself. But he knows the price
of the inner life, and beneath his affectation of the lettered adolescent,
he is full of a child-like need for affection. He already has character;
may he be gently handled![6]

As with Claudel, the poems of the adolescent Perse establish
the theme and manner of his later works. They present an
awareness of the concrete world and a precise and evocative
imagery.

A poet is made from many experiences. Not unusual is the
fact that those of childhood leave a permanent impression. Both
Claudel and Perse cast their impressions through the prism of
their intellect, memory, and sensitivity, and the poet was born.
Family relationships and childhood surroundings represent only
a part of the fabric from which the poet is made. Even the most
precocious lyricist must have formal training. Mention has al-
ready been made of Perse's studies with the botanist, Duss. This

5. Saint-John Perse, *Oeuvre Poétique*, 2 vols. (Paris, 1960). In references
from this work the volume is indicated by roman numerals and the page
by arabic numerals.

6. Paul Claudel, Francis Jammes, and Gabriel Frizeau, *Correspondance,
1897–1938* (Paris, 1952), p. 102.

was the beginning of an education which evolved into an encyclopedic knowledge of the world. According to Alain Bosquet, Perse studied geology under a follower of Eduard Suess at Bordeaux. Suess believed that intuition and the poetic vision prevailed over empirical truth, and in order to broaden the dimensions of his geological theories, he called upon supernatural entities. These studies formed the basis for Perse's ideas about humanity and its future and the planet Earth as finite in time and space. The epic of this planet would be entitled, *Vents*.[7] Claudel's studies in the physical and natural sciences were less felicitous. He had no affinity for them. On the insistence of his professors, however, he did learn optics and natural history. Particularly under the influence of one of his teachers, a professor Mangin, Claudel developed an interest in natural history and maintained a taste for it.[8] Years later, he would read several volumes of Fabre's *Souvenirs entomologiques* and other scientific treatises. He counseled Frizeau to read the work, and indicated that *Souvenirs* gave him ideas for the *Connaissance du Temps* and *Traité de la Co-Naissance au monde et de soi-même*: "It is intoxicating reading by the quantity of ideas that it creates, and for my part, that is where I found the suggestion for my two Theses."[9] Both poets distinguished themselves as *lycéens*, Perse at Pau, and Claudel at Louis-le-Grand. Each received the *prix de discours français*. Perse received Fabre's *Lectures sur la Botanique* as the prize in natural sciences at the Lycée of La-Pointe-à-Pitre in 1898.

After studying law, both men decided on a career in foreign affairs. Claudel's "passion de l'univers," his desire to extend his knowledge of the physical world, and his eagerness to travel figured in his choice of a diplomatic career. Perse was influenced in his choice by Philippe Berthelot and by Claudel who dissuaded the young man from becoming a colonial magistrate when he was yet uncertain about the diplomatic corps.[10] The

7. Alain Bosquet, *Saint-John Perse* (Paris, 1953), p. 92.
8. *Mémoires Improvisés*, p. 7.
9. *Correspondance*, p. 63.
10. Claudel met Perse in 1905 at the home of Francis Jammes. Their friendship was maintained through correspondence and infrequent encounters for many years. Claudel's interest in Perse is attested to by the

careers of these men and their personal interests took them to many parts of the world. Their work and their contacts with different cultures and civilizations were continuing processes in the making of the poet. Perse does not acknowledge any liaison between Alexis Saint-Léger Léger, the diplomat, and Saint-John Perse, the poet.[11] However, since each experience is bound within one's consciousness, its effect is inevitable.

In several works, particularly in *Contacts et Circonstances*, Claudel presents a vivid and moving description of his discovery of Rimbaud and his subsequent conversion the same year. The effects of these events reverberated through the years and shaped and gave substance to Claudel's poetic production. His objective, in December, 1886, of writing "quelques exercices décadents" grew into a revelation, a vision, and a literary production of gigantic proportions. In the case of Perse, the event which served as the catalytic agent (although he had written and published a major work by 1924), was World War II. In 1940, he found himself an exile on alien shores, divested of citizenship, honors, and possessions. Christian Murciaux evaluates his position: "The effort of adaptation which a new life in a foreign country demands only rendered more persuasive the interior voice and exigency which arose from an age in revolution, a rejected continent, abandoned cities, silent ports, empty reservoirs, pillaged libraries, profaned temples and altars. It was the role of an exile to reestablish all of that."[12] Astounded by cataclysmic events in Europe, personal loss, and an intuition of further catastrophe in the making, Saint-John Perse looked aside from the brooding nostalgia of previous years and mankind in the evolution of civilizations. His vision became one of interiorization—man's inward journey and destiny.

In an abbreviated manner, the implications of family and heritage, malaise occasioned by displacement, important formal studies, choice of careers, and traumatic experiences are suggested as forces in the formation of the poet. That poets are born is altogether possible; that poets are shaped by circum-

---

fact that there are twenty-seven references to him in the *Correspondance*.

11. Christian Murciaux, *Saint-John Perse* (Paris, 1960), p. 7.

12. Ibid., p. 22.

stances is undeniable. The poem itself is born from the conjunction of personality and experience, modified by intellect and circumstance.

III. The Mission of the Poet

Most poets agree that the poetic creation results from the harmonious coordination of impression and expression. The concern here is with the "why" of expression, not particularly the force which makes expression inevitable; rather, the purpose of expression. In short, What needs does the poet fulfill? What is his function?

The mission of the poet is sacerdotal and secular in nature. His task is that of elucidation and communication. Elucidation is necessary because the world itself is one gigantic symbol whose components are all created things, animate and inanimate. The mallarméen dictum of the symbolistic nature of the universe is expanded by Claudel in accordance with Thomist doctrine. In his *Traité de la Co-Naissance*, he writes: "Chaque homme a été créé pour être le témoin et l'acteur d'un certain spectacle, pour en déterminer en lui le sens."[1] Among created beings, God has chosen witnesses who bear testimony and restore reality to

1. "Art Poétique," *Oeuvre Poétique* (Paris, 1957), p. 190.

things in various ways, according to their order.[2] In the "Magnificat," Claudel declares the fact of his having been chosen: "Vous m'avez appelé par mon nom / Comme quelqu'un qui le connaît, vous m'avez choisi entre tous ceux de mon âge" (III, 249). By intuition, the poet realizes that he is interwoven with the surrounding phenomena, that he is tuned in on the creative act, and hence must himself become creator and interpreter.[3] The poet then carries out his role of conquering the world through comprehension of it, and subsequently the expression of this comprehension through the written word. In the whole body of Claudel's writings are found the tenets of his purpose of expression stated in philosophical or lyrical form. He, as poet, creates universal harmony using as substance his cognitive and non-cognitive experience.

The why of Claudel's poetic expression stems from his conversion and his desire to complete his personal evolution in a God-centered universe. To Joseph de Tonquédec, in a letter dated June 13, 1917, he wrote that his profound concern was for his own evangelization: "When I write, the idea of the intrinsic beauty of what I do or of the pleasure that I can gain is completely foreign to me. For me, poetry is the expression of strong and profound sentiments, and secondly the means of this campaign of progressive evangelization of all of the areas of my intelligence and of all of the powers of my soul which I have been trying to pursue . . . since the day when I was converted."[4]

The expression of the poet thus fulfills initially a personal need by providing the means for an interior dialogue in order to resolve uncertainties, and for the external representation of experience. The poet not only re-creates the universe, he re-creates himself. (The *Art Poétique*, written at a time of intense personal stress, gave direction to Claudel's interiorization and resolution to his dilemma.) Pierre Angers in his *Commentaire à l'Art Poétique de Paul Claudel* affirms that: "The poet of the universe is at the same time the poet of himself. By his creative activities, man 'reforges his person.' In contact with the world,

2. Ibid., p. 188.
3. Ibid., p. 190.
4. *L'Oeuvre de Paul Claudel* (Paris, 1927), p. 196.

he tests and edifies himself."[5] Comprehension of the material world is not only the means of rendering homage to the Creator, it also leads to the mastery of one's self and to a "conversion still more complete, thanks to which the Kingdom of God established in the soul extends its conquests to all of the interior regions."[6]

In his correspondence with Jacques Rivière, Claudel explained that religion does not create new faculties in the individual, rather, it makes possible the usage of those which he does possess. On the purpose of expression, he said that Shakespeare, Dostoievsky, Rubens, Titian, and Wagner were not working primarily to produce art. Their objective was "to rid themselves of their burden, to cast outside this great bundle of living things, *opus non factum*: and not to color on the outside a cold and artificial design."[7] The artist through his art is thus unified and can more accurately imitate the gestures of the Creator in establishing harmony and unity: "Car qu'est aucune prise et jouissance et propriété et aménagement / Auprès de l'intelligence du poëte qui fait de plusieurs choses ensemble une seule avec lui, / Puisque comprendre, c'est refaire / La chose même que l'on a prise avec soi" (III, 261).

Claudel's conception of the poet as God's witness and interpreter of creation is not that of Perse. In fact, God is a word "religiously" avoided by him, according to Claudel who wonders what he sought beyond the barriers of the incommensurable: "Et cependant, conduit par le soleil au rebours de ce souffle tantôt violent, et tantôt perfide, et tantôt méditatif, qu'allait-il chercher au delà de toute barrière, qu'allait-il demander aux réservoirs de l'incommensurable?"[8] But for Perse, there was no religious preoccupation, no anguish, no concern about another universe presided over by a Judge charged with remedying the injustices of this world. Perse does, however, concur with Claudel as to the immediate and personal needs fulfilled

5. (Paris, 1949), p. 40.
6. Ibid., p. 42.
7. Jacques Rivière and Paul Claudel, *Correspondance, 1907–1914* (Paris, 1926), p. 248.
8. *Oeuvres Complètes* (Paris, 1950–), "Un Poème de Saint-John Perse," Vol. XVIII, *Accompagnements* (1961), p. 239.

by expression. As an exile, figuratively and literally, he presents in all of his writings evidence of the inner tensions which possessed him. His work is the chronicle of an inward voyage whose goal is the resolution of personal turmoil and the deciphering of exterior chaos. Monique Parent describes the three themes of *Anabase* as that of a military conquest, a poetic adventure, and the human adventure. It is the poetic adventure which leads the poet to the discovery and conquest of himself: "The role of the poet is to go thus to the discovery of himself and of the world, without thinking any more of stopping or of building, and his activity resembles more that of the mariner than that of the architect."[9] The interiorization on the part of Perse allowed him to identify the nature of his distress and bewilderment. Parent indicates the scope of his confrontation with himself as reflected in *Images*: "The human being, grappling with the basic realities of life: space, time, the elements, suffering, the presence of others, takes possession by degrees of his inner life, of his spiritual power."[10] Because of his deep sensitivity, Perse had to express lyrically his journey which is also that of humanity.

Perse further concurs with Claudel when he sees the poet as bearing the burden of eternity and of humanity. He feels that poetry must fathom the human mystery and concern itself with man in the fullness of his being. Also, he affirms that in modern poetry there is no place for anything purely aesthetic: though related to beauty, beauty is not its goal. In *Poésie*, he discusses the nature of poetry, and defines the scope of his own work: "Se refusant à dissocier l'art de la vie, ni de l'amour la connaissance, elle est action, elle est passion, elle est puissance . . . Et c'est d'une même étreinte, comme d'une seule grande strophe vivante, qu'elle embrasse au présent tout le passé et l'avenir, l'humain avec le surhumain, et tout l'espace planétaire avec l'espace universel" (p. 16).

The conquest of self seems therefore to be the first perceptible role of Claudel and Perse in the expression of their innermost thoughts. The re-creation of self assumes several aspects. The poet's effort to create a new self results in his detachment, figu-

9. *Saint-John Perse et quelques devanciers* (Paris, 1960), p. 204.
10. Ibid., p. 240.

ratively, from the commonplace, the banalities of existence. The lack of self-unity in Claudel occasioned by the solitude of childhood, the spiritual bewilderment of young manhood, the effort to choose between art and religion after his conversion, the illicit love affair for four years in China, all of these critical periods during his maturation made imperative the ordering of his inner world. In "L'Esprit et l'Eau," he confesses his need by acknowledging his desolation:

> Mon Dieu,
> Je me vois et je me juge, et je n'ai plus aucun prix pour moi-même.
> Vous m'avez donné la vie: je vous la rends; je préfère que vous repreniez tout.
> Je me vois enfin! et j'en ai désolation, et la douleur intérieure en moi ouvre tout comme un oeil liquide.
> O mon Dieu, je ne veux plus rien, et je vous rends tout, et rien n'a plus de prix pour moi,
> Et je ne vois plus que ma misère, et mon néant, et ma privation, et cela du moins est à moi! (II, 246)

The Muse cries to Claudel to liberate himself before he attempts to liberate men and unify creation: "Libère-toi toi-même! Réunisseur de tous les hommes, réunis-toi toi-même! / Sois un seul esprit! sois une seule intention!" (IV, 275).

The acknowledgment of personal responsibility for his malaise is absent from the writings of Perse. Inherent factors and his reaction to external events certainly contributed to his state of mind. His temperament, his personal fortunes, and his contemplation resulted in an inner dissension which he sought to resolve in poetic expression. This dissension he sought to dominate before trying to comprehend the turmoil of humanity. A sort of reconciliation is achieved in *Exil*.

Poetry, as has been indicated, has a broader function than that of a personal panacea for the poet. Although he acquires an inner unity and self-fulfillment, his is a broader mission as witness, creator, spokesman, and interpreter. This further function of the poet is necessary when one considers the poet's concept of the human condition.

For Saint-John Perse, the world is man-centered, and it is the poet who occupies the most elevated rank in the hierarchy of humanity, and who must therefore fulfill its needs. It is he who will serve as the spokesman for man. In "Amitié du Prince," Perse speaks of the poet as "Prince vêtu de tes sentences," "Nourri des souffles de la terre," "docile aux souffles de la terre." He delineates his role as follows: "Tu es le Guérisseur et l'Assesseur et l'Enchanteur aux sources de l'esprit! Car ton pouvoir au coeur de l'homme est une chose étrange et ton aisance est grande parmi nous. / J'ai vu le signe sur ton front et j'ai considéré ton rôle parmi nous" (I, 94).

The poet as spokesman expresses that which for ordinary man is inexpressible. His is a vision which encompasses the real and the symbolic and gives purpose to an apparently meaningless succession of days. In this manner, he hopes to alleviate the anguish of man. Perse, endowed with intuition and reason, considers the world as a text written in a code which can be deciphered by the poet, "environné des signes les plus fastes." In the deciphering, Perse's quest is for the "souffle" which he discerns as being embedded in the most violent aspects of the elemental forces of the universe: storms, hurricanes, blizzards, typhoons, lightning, and the raging sea. The turbulent forces of the elements, glorified in *Vents, Pluies, Neiges,* and *Amers,* mirror the disquiet in Perse's soul. An awareness of this makes possible the establishment of a bond between himself and the universe. Because of this bond, he is led to believe that reality itself is chaotic and violent, yet fragile, ephemeral, and transient. The sea, representing "toute licence, toute naissance," is his most powerful and frequent symbol. In *Amers,* he expresses this preference: "Pour nous le Continent de mer, non point la terre nuptiale et son parfum de fenugrec; pour nous le libre lieu de mer, non ce versant de l'homme usuel aveuglé d'astres domestiques" (II, 202). Representing, as it does, violence, change, movement, space, the unfathomable, the unknown and unknowable, the sea for Perse is the poem seeking expression and release as does the soul itself. It is here that he is most cognizant of the "Souffle Originel." As Wallace Fowlie asserts, the poetry of Perse reveals his desire to reach the inaccessible source.[11]

---

11. "The Art of Saint-John Perse," *Poetry,* 79 (1951–52), 35.

As an alien, with the "ferment du vieux monde" on his lips, he was representative of all men figuratively exiled by the harshness of life. It is for these men that he speaks, that they might not despair, despite exile and the precariousness of life.[12] In the wastelands of exile, his purpose was to create a poem "né de rien, un grand poème fait de rien." To himself he says: "Honore, ô Prince, ton exil! / Et soudain tout m'est force et présence, où fume encore le thème du néant" (I, 172–73).

During the years of exile, 1940 to 1945, Perse, by means of observation, contemplation and meditation, became profoundly conscious of man's condition and the poet's obligation to mankind. In the poem *Vents*, these two themes are dominant in the panoramic canvas of America and the New World. The poet, refreshed by the storms, compares himself to the Shaman who "has eaten the rice of the dead." Thus informed, he is prepared to shout words of encouragement to the living. He invokes the favor of the gods for the power of divination in the poem (II, 14–15). Again he acknowledges his duty: "O vous que rafraîchit l'orage . . . fraîcheur et gage de fraîcheur . . . / Repris aux dieux votre visage, au feu des forges votre éclat, / Voici que vous logez de ce côté du Siècle où vous aviez vocation. / . . . Et si l'homme de talent préfère la roseraie et le jeu de clavecin, il sera dévoré par les chiens" (II, 31–32).

Unlike those looking backward and dreaming dreams of the past, the poet wishes to look ahead by dissolving his sadness in the new wine and joining those men "assaillis du dieu. Hommes nourris au vin nouveau et comme percé d'éclairs" (II, 28). Thus renewed, the poet turns toward the business of man, he listens to the cry of the living: "Car c'est de l'homme qu'il s'agit, dans sa présence humaine; et d'un agrandissement de l'oeil aux plus hautes mers intérieures. / Se hâter! se hâter! témoignage pour l'homme!" (II, 77). And the poet forsakes his grand isolation and establishes himself with men of patience, of gentleness and smiles, men of all kinds and conditions—the workers, the dreamers, the thinkers: well-diggers, astrologers, cobblers, financiers, sculptors, navigators, radiologists, engineers, and mathematicians:

12. Alain Bosquet, *Saint-John Perse* (Paris, 1953), p. 47.

> ... Avec son peuple de servants, avec son peuple de suivants,
> et tout son train de hardes dans le vent, ô sourire, ô douceur,
> Le Poète lui-même à la coupée du Siècle!
> —Accueil sur la chaussée des hommes, et le vent à cent
> lieues courbant l'herbe nouvelle.
> Car c'est de l'homme qu'il s'agit, et de son renouement.
> Quelqu'un au monde n'élèvera-t-il la voix?
> Témoignage pour l'homme ...
> Que le Poète se fasse entendre, et qu'il dirige le jugement!
> (II, 80)

Placing himself thus among men, a partner to his sorrow, the poet offers hope by affirming the solidarity of man.

Claudel's awareness of his mission to mankind is less abstract. Just as his entire life was dedicated to clearing a pathway for himself to God, in like manner did he devote himself to illuminating man's journey to salvation. Numerous are the instances in which he proselytized among his contemporaries, including Perse himself. In the early years after his conversion, Claudel's main concern was with his personal salvation. The philosophical meditations of *Art Poétique*, the lyrical expression of the *Cinq Grandes Odes*, and the poignant revelations of *Partage de Midi* are all reflections of the same confusion, doubt, guilt, confession, and repentance experienced by Claudel. Yet, even while entangled in this web of personal dilemma, by means of correspondence and conversation, he was endeavoring to bring men to God.

Many of the letters to Jacques Rivière present a course of action for men engulfed in doubt and desirous of resolving their "combat spirituel." In a letter dated May 25, 1907, from Tien-Tsin, Claudel makes clear his objective: "It is for me the primary and most pleasant of duties to try to do a little good for young men struggling in the same crisis through which I formerly passed."[13] He directs his attention particularly to young men because he feels that it is in the twentieth year that they experience an upheaval which determines the future course of their lives.

From time to time it seems that Claudel rejects and resists any involvement with man as when he is stirred by "l'ébranle-

13. *Correspondance*, p. 59.

ment de la cohorte Olympique." At this moment of transport, he cries: "Que m'importent tous les hommes à présent! Ce n'est pas pour eux que je suis fait, mais pour le / Transport de cette mesure sacrée!" (IV, 264). On the other hand, in the dialogue between himself and "la Muse qui est la Grâce," he feels that he would like to avoid the winged flight of Pegasus and sing of the works of man because the writer's duty is to keep the accounts of all humanity (IV, 266). This song of mankind is to be done in the style of an "art studieux." The Muse reproaches him for this kind of clerical study, this secular attachment. He is invited to imbibe of that wine which causes one to see things as they are and as they are not. In order to transform the world, he must himself be transformed by drinking of the celestial wine: "Fi de vous, ô chiches jours terrestres! O noces! ô prémisses de l'esprit! bois de ce vin non fermenté seulement! / Avance-toi et vois l'éternel matin, la terre et la mer sous le soleil du matin, comme quelqu'un qui paraît devant le trône de Dieu!" (IV, 269). In response, Claudel beseeches the Muse not to tempt him with an illumination too brilliant for the sons of the Earth. He is still lost in the shadows and believes that he has been placed on earth in order to endure restraint, obscurity, and violence in the midst of other men (IV, 271). The Muse then threatens him with sorrow if he refuses the libation of joy. Anguished, the poet reiterates that every being, every man, every voice is essential for his personal fulfillment, and that he can only respond to the Muse's call with all beings who surround him. The Muse identifies herself as being Grace which chose him even before he was born: ". . . c'est moi qui t'ai choisi avant que tu ne sois né. / Entre tous les êtres qui vivent, je suis la parole de grâce qui est adressée à toi seul" (IV, 275). The invitation follows for him to liberate and unify himself. But there is the final rejection by one who has bitten of the dust and retains its savor, who has tasted of blood and refuses to be nourished by honey, who has loved a human being and remains entrapped for all time (IV, 276).

The doubt and the guilt and the yearning encompassed in the fourth ode reflect a struggle with a personal emotion, a search for a direction in his art, and a clarification of his duty to bewildered mankind. This is his final cry of revolt because previously he had acknowledged in the "Magnificat" that he would devote his life to communicating the divine message to mankind. His capitulation to his mission as witness, spokesman, interpreter is summarized in the fifth ode, "La Maison Fermée." Of Claudel's mission, P. Lorigiola says: ". . . he must reveal to men the obscure summits by which the earth is in contact with Heaven."[14]

14. "Les Grandes Odes de Claudel," *Les Etudes Classiques,* 27 (April 1959), 153–54.

IV. The Inception of the Poem

Whence comes the inspiration for poetic expression? The poet's concept of his mission and its fulfillment are circumscribed by the origin of his inspiration. Claudel's inspiration derives from a gift of grace; that of Perse from an intuition of a chaotic universe. This gift, this intuition placed both writers in a lyrical state of mind defined by Parent as a state of tension which has to be expressed. The tension develops after a violent rupture on the part of the poet from that which is the artist's usual state of consciousness, a departure from his normal mental state of being.

Claudel's rupture is from worldly concerns and an unfortunate personal involvement; that of Perse is from a somnolent, nostalgic, even bitter contemplation of a lost paradise. The breaking away from one's normal self seems to confer a sort of anonymity on the poetic creation. It is as though the poet becomes endowed with what Valéry calls "spiritual energy" which transforms him and thrusts him into a poetic state. Speaking of the reader's concept of the poet, Valéry writes: ". . . for it can

[25]

only be an exceptional form of stimulus that simultaneously produces the exaltation of our sensibility, our intellect, our memory, and our powers of verbal action, so rarely granted to us in the ordinary course of life."[1]

The inception of the poem derives from three conditions of the poet: 1. the thrust of his mind toward a state of inspiration; 2. the separation from his normal state, accompanied by an eruption; 3. the new self created by the separation. Perse's arrival at the first state resulted from continuous observation, reflection, and contemplation. Observation as a child of the splendors of the physical world led to wonder and amazement. During his childhood, it was the sea which was to him the most impressive aspect of observable phenomena. In *Pour fêter une Enfance*, its mystery is expressed in the phrase, "Alors une mer plus crédule et hantée d'invisibles départs" (I, 26). This sea on which Princes walked was pictured as pale meadows of naked water (I, 27). In the morning light it resembled the calm and majesty of a holy day on which sleep assumed the posture of a deity on bended knees (I, 27). The sea, in its promise of revelation of its secrets beyond the horizon, has magnetic force on the man who in his dreams "s'achemine vers la mer": ". . . Tout l'intime de l'eau se resonge en silence aux contrées de la toile" (I, 44). The brilliant light of the tropics also dazzled the child who, in retrospect, wrote: "Et tout n'était que règnes et confins de lueurs" (I, 21). The light created for him a kingdom in which he conceived of himself as a body divested of shadow. A subliminal inspiration was probably already at work as he gazed at the broad expanse of water and experienced the tropical brilliance of Guadeloupe.

There can be no chronological tracing of the growth of inspiration, but it is impossible to ignore the impact of later experiences in the distant corners of the world on the inquiring spirit of Perse. His travels took him across deserts, oceans, and densely populated areas. Thus he had occasion to observe the condition of man and the cultures of mankind. The continuing exposure to that which he had known intimately as a child made

1. Paul Valéry, "Poetry and Abstract Thought," *The Art of Poetry*, trans. Denise Folliot (New York, 1958), p. 79.

him the contemplative stranger described in *Anabase*, filled with new thoughts, traveling the paths of silence, seeking answers to the mystery of the world. Contemplating the vastness of the universe in the overwhelming silence of a literal and figurative exile, Perse was the man of language, grappling with the sources of his god (II, 54). The agitation experienced by the poet was that of the spirit, scarred by exile, yet questing like the winds over the faces of the living, throughout the entire world of things. He invoked the divination of the elements: "Divination par l'eau du ciel . . . / Et de tels rites furent favorables. J'en userai. Faveur du dieu sur mon poème! Et qu'elle ne vienne à lui manquer! / 'Favorisé du songe favorable' fut l'expression choisie pour exalter la condition du sage. Et le poète encore trouve recours dans son poème" (II, 15). The sea, the light, the deserts, and the winds quickened Perse's apperception of the source. In "Les Tragédiennes sont venues" of *Amers*, the poet begs of the sea inspiration for new, strong, and beautiful works which will create in man the desire to live like men. He desires works of a lofty style and a broader meter for the narration of the seen and the unseen (II, 178–79).

In describing the object of Perse's quest, Claude Vigée is of the opinion that the fervor of the poet was aroused by a wave of energy similar to the life-giving breath, the "souffle vivifiant" of the first pages of Genesis. This energetic wave, resembling the attack of a predatory eagle, imprinted its movement on the mind of the solitary exile in the manner of a violent rape: ". . . elle prend possession de l'esprit dans un rapt."[2] This invasion of the soul is similar to the "rapt sec" of Claudel's which he describes in "L'Esprit et l'Eau": "Soudain l'Esprit de nouveau, soudain le souffle de nouveau, / Soudain le coup sourd au coeur, soudain le mot donné, soudain le souffle de l'Esprit, le rapt sec, soudain la possession de l'Esprit!" (p. 234). The rape of the soul indicates a separation, a transcendence of that which was, be it memory, intellect, conscience, logic, or reason. In *Vents*, Perse expresses this idea when he says: "Il n'y a plus pour nous d'entente avec cela qui fut" (II, 109).

There is nothing staid, calm, or restful in the works of Perse.

2. *Révolte et Louanges* (Paris, 1962), p. 203.

Almost always he speaks of violence, force, fury, eruption, defiance, and struggle. His writings represent poetic anger describing both the delights and the ordure of creation (II, 49). That "la colère poétique" should be evident in Perse derives from the shock of separation on his spirit. The encounter with the god causes him to reject reveling in sadness: "Qu'ils n'aillent point dire: tristesse . . . s'y plaisant—dire: tristesse . . . s'y logeant, comme aux ruelles de l'amour. / Interdiction d'en vivre! Interdiction faite au poète, faite aux fileuses de mémoire" (II, 82). He casts aside logic: "Je te licencierai, logique, où s'estropiaient nos bêtes à l'entrave" (II, 83). He desires the blurring of the clear eye of reason: "Brouille-toi, vision, où s'entêtait l'homme de raison" (II, 82). Stripped of the encumbrances of memory, intellect, conscience, logic, the poet is at the noon-time of being, free of his shadow, "à la limite de son bien" (II, 317). In the poetic state in which he finds himself, Perse is intoxicated with the possibilities of re-creating, having drunk of the new wine: "D'autres ont bu le vin nouveau dans les fontaines peintes au minium. Et de ceux-là nous fûmes. Et la tristesse que nous fûmes s'en aille au vin nouveau des hommes comme aux fêtes du vent!" (II, 28).

Assailed by the god, the poet has acquired strength and an "oeil occulte." The dimensions of his vision and his comprehension are unlimited. For him, the gods who march in the wind will make known the origin and meaning of act (II, 29). The quickened illumination of his soul enables him to seize completely the thing itself at the point of being (II, 86). Perse describes the poet still with us, among the men of his time, infested with the dream, infected by the divine, attentive to his lucidity, jealous of his authority, and maintaining the breadth and depth of his vision (II, 86–87).

There are close parallels between Perse and Claudel in the thrust toward the source of inspiration, the resultant separation from self, and the creation of a new being in a poetic state. Perse found inspiration in the elements themselves as the fount of the original source. Claudel, through the elements, saw God the Creator, the First Cause, and subsequently received grace and inspiration. Like Perse, he followed the path of meditation to discover the secret of the universe. Of this aspect of the poet, Tonquédec writes:

However the ardent contemplative person that is Paul Claudel is not satisfied to listen to nature while dreaming and to gather symbols from the surface of things. For him, it is a question of understanding by meditation the secret of the Universe. Liking it for itself, he scrutinizes it relentlessly, with a jealous and unsatiated avidity. . . . He is a philosopher, a tenacious metaphysicist. He examines reality in order to seize and touch its foundations.[3]

Claudel's sojourn in the Orient was propitious for him to formulate, through contemplation and meditation, certain ideas basic to his metaphysics. Submerged in a new culture and exposed to a geography radically different from his own, he saw in Asia the primordial face of nature and could begin to sense the essence of creation, the original unity of matter. In *Connaissance de l'Est*, he describes this vast continent as "the Earth of the Earth, Asia, mother of all men, central, solid, primordial! O the abundance of her bosom!" (*Oeuvre Poétique*, p. 62). He was enraptured by the magnificent colors of the dawn, wondered about the meaning of such glory, and marveled at being afforded such joy: "But that which troubles me as a lover, that which makes me tremble in my flesh is the *intention* of glory of this, it is my *admission*, it is the advancement of this joy to meet me!" (*Oeuvre Poétique*, p. 69).

In a letter to Abbé Brémond, Claudel defines three types of inspiration which are possible if it is recognized that the imagination and sensibility supersede the secondary supporting and organizing force of reason. The imagination must have a vivid conception of the object to be realized, and the sensibility, stimulated by varied activity, must be desirous of expressing the concept in question.[4] The first type of inspiration is a more or less natural aptness to express in words the imagination's concepts. The born poet must have something within to be kindled by the breath of inspiration. Claudel describes inspiration in the second sense as real inspiration. The poet finds himself in a cre-

3. Joseph de Tonquédec, *L'Oeuvre de Paul Claudel* (Paris, 1927), pp. 23–24.
4. "Lettre à l'Abbé Brémond sur l'inspiration poétique," *Positions et Propositions* (Paris, 1928), I, 94.

ative state as a result of an inner rhythmic excitation which leads him to choose the exact word, the necessary balance to express the imagined concept. The concordance and sharpening of all faculties make such expression possible.

A discourse on "Poetry and Abstract Thought," made in 1939 by Paul Valéry, includes an experience on the part of the writer recounted in order to differentiate between the poetic state and the production of a work. While taking a walk for a change of atmosphere, a rhythm seized him as though it were an outside force. The first rhythm was followed and combined with a second. The combined rhythms harmonized with his walking movement and a spontaneous song was created from within. Overwhelmed by the composition, Valéry felt that grace had been bestowed on the wrong person, since he was not a musician. Such a poetic state he considers involuntary, accidental, and ephemeral; yet Valéry acknowledges that there is reciprocity and synchronization between forms of action and mental creation.[5] This experience of Valéry falls generally into the second category of inspiration described by Claudel because of the nature of the creative impulse which is grounded in emotion. As Claudel's orator was astonished by his flow of eloquence,[6] so was Valéry amazed by his creation. The creative impulse is centered in emotion, self-engendered according to Claudel, spontaneous by Valéry's account. Before the word, Claudel says, there is a certain intensity, quality, and proportion of spiritual tension.[7] Speaking to Amrouche on the subject of *Partage de Midi*, Claudel mentions the unbidden inspiration: "There are works which come to the mind of an artist whence no one knows, and which he would be very embarrassed to explain with his own psychology."[8]

The third sense of the word inspiration, in Claudel's view, centers on the use of words which reveal the real nature of things and do not simply designate them. The poet uses words not for utility's sake, "but in order to constitute with all of

5. Valéry, *The Art of Poetry*, pp. 60–62.
6. *Positions et Propositions*, I, 96–97.
7. "Réflexions et propositions sur le vers français," *Positions et Propositions*, I, 10.
8. *Mémoires Improvisés* (Paris, 1954), p. 182.

these sonorous phantoms which the word puts at his disposal, a picture both intelligible and delightful."[9] The image thus created represents "la chose pure" which is a partial image of God. Claudel's inspiration derives both from his sense of "la chose pure" and an inner excitation. About the inner emotion, he feels that a work is not truly a work of art unless it comes from the depths of the author's spirit and even "de ses boyaux."[10]

Seduced by the Spirit, Claudel experienced "le rapt sec" which separated him from that which he was. It was after a prolonged and silent contemplation of the sea that the poet was assailed by the Spirit. In "L'Esprit et l'Eau," water symbolizes the spirit which binds us to God. The ode itself is compared to the sea, the sea of all human utterance. The sea is the incomprehensible element in which mortal man seeks something solid to which he may cling. Divine grace, that which man must seek, is the basis of Claudel's inspiration.

In the first ode in which Claudel saluted the nine Muses whose creative presence was necessary, he had described the new poet who is suddenly overwhelmed by an explosive inspiration and is compelled to speak. This is "le rapt sec" which has liberated Claudel from terrestrial concerns and made him one with the creative liquid element of the spirit:

> Mais que m'importent à présent vos empires, et tout ce qui meurt,
> Et vous autres que j'ai laissés, votre voie hideuse là-bas!
> Puisque je suis libre! que m'importent vos arrangements cruels? puisque moi du moins je suis libre! puisque j'ai trouvé! puisque moi du moins je suis dehors!
> Puisque je n'ai plus ma place avec les choses créées, mais ma part avec ce qui les crée, l'esprit liquide et lascif! (II, 235)

In a much later discussion on the nature of the spirit in *Présence et Prophétie*, Claudel poses this question: "ne dit-on pas de l'esprit qu'il se meut, qu'il vole, qu'il plane, qu'il fulgure, qu'il conquiert pied à pied une connaissance . . . ?"[11] The invasion of the spirit, more penetrating than any liquid element, enabled Claudel to recognize "le souffle secret," the creative force,

9. *Positions et Propositions*, I, 98.
10. *Mémoires Improvisés*, p. 183.
11. (Paris, 1942), p. 250.

and thus discern and express the meaning of action and visible phenomena.

The rupture brought about by "le rapt sec" created a new being reunited with the source. Claudel desires clarification and the dissolution of execrable shadows so that he may move closer to God. He beseeches Him to deliver him from himself, from the slavery and weight of inert matter, and from the corruptibility of inert water. In a lyrical outpouring of memory, Claudel acknowledges his past errors of the flesh and repents having allowed this obstacle to separate him from the Creator. Of his body, he says: "Mais je ne puis forcer en cette vie / Vers vous à cause de mon corps" (II, 239). The renouncement of self has caused the poet to be endowed with new qualities. The new quality of double vision enables him to recognize the divinity in the temporal. God, for him, is as visible in this world as in the other; he has a total perception of the world in a single glance; everything has acquired measure and proportion in his sight; in short, a new world has been revealed to him. Wherever he turns his head, he envisages the immense octave of Creation (II, 240).

The newly-acquired double vision is accompanied by a sharpening of all of the poet's faculties: "Je sens, je flaire, je débrouille, je dépiste, je respire avec un certain sens / La chose comment elle est faite!" (II, 237–38). Claudel's sense of "la chose pure," brought about by the "rapt sec" of the spirit, leads to a greater creative ability. A life-creating light illuminates his intelligence and enables him to bring to each thing its deliverance, revealing its nature as a work and the expression of Eternity. With the voice of the poet, Claudel makes use of eternal words in directing men to God; and he contrasts the eternal nature of his verses with the ephemeral quality of the leaf: "Ainsi la voix avec qui de vous je fais des mots éternels! je ne puis rien nommer que d'éternel. / La feuille jaunit et le fruit tombe, mais la feuille dans mes vers ne périt pas, / Ni le fruit mûr, ni la rose entre les roses! / Elle périt, mais son nom dans l'esprit qui est mon esprit ne périt plus" (II, 242–43). Claudel seeks a totally intelligible word for his poem. God, who breathed on chaos and created order, and put life into the molded clay, has similarly placed within him the same spirit of creation. It is this spirit which has made it possible for him to unlock the mystery of the divine handiwork.

Claudel and Perse evolved into the poetic state as a result of bewilderment, curiosity, unhappiness, a confrontation with self, a rupture with the past, and a subsequent exaltation of the sensibilities and of the intellect. Both poets sought a revelation of the "souffle originel"; both experienced an invasion of the creative spirit; both sought to express the meaning of the visible world.

V. Re-Creation
of the Universe—Perse

Claudel's and Perse's vision of the universe is filtered through the prism of personal experience, inner tumult, and creative imagination. By their intellect they were able to give order and form to the vision. The dimensions of their intellect reflect their passion to know and understand the visible world. It was this concrete world, widely experienced by both, which became for them the matter of poetry. By synthesizing that which was perceived, they established a unity of meaning. Perse was guided in his synthesis by an intuition of intellect, Claudel by an intuition of faith.

Perse addressed himself to the "monde entier des choses" since it was necessary to consider the universe in its totality in order to ascertain its origins and establish the harmony of its seemingly disparate segments. His curiosity, sensibility, and intellect enabled him to encompass the conventional and unconventional aspects of nature and humanity in his poetic world. His works consist of multiple references to natural phenomena, to singular aspects of man's culture, past and present, and to obscure phases in the evolution of civilizations. Such facts are presented in more than an allusive or referential form. They constitute the substance of the poem.

Enumerations of the occupations and activities of man, detailed precisely and specifically in all of their facets, attest to Perse's humane interests and knowledge. His vocabulary of the flora and fauna of all lands is encyclopedic in breadth. His allusions to the culture and civilizations of all of the ages of mankind bespeak unusual experience and information. In short, Perse has a close acquaintance with "le monde entier des choses." The manner in which he reads this world of things is what constitutes his poetic genius. He makes use of his knowledge aesthetically, lexically, and philosophically to create his universe. It is language applied to specifics in an artistic way that transfigures and illuminates the world of things. At this point, however, the concern is with his philosophic creation, though it is almost impossible to separate the three points of view which are basically interdependent.

Through observation and experience, Perse was immediately aware of the turbulence of the natural elements, the chaos and disorder in the affairs of men, and the repeated cycles of destructive force in the history of civilizations. It was in the turbulence of the physical world, repeated in human activity, that Perse discerned the creative forces of the universe. This idea of the violent manifestations of the elements as creative forces is equated with the role of the elements in artistic creativity. In *Exil*, he describes the ever-present clamor, splendor, and furor: ". . . Toujours il y eut cette clameur, toujours il y eut cette grandeur, / Cette chose errante par le monde, cette haute transe par le monde, et sur toutes grèves de ce monde, du même souffle proférée, la même vague proférant / Une seule et longue phrase sans césure à jamais inintelligible . . ." (I, 171–72). In the same manner that this continuous, nameless, incomprehensible force creates and re-creates the universe, the poetry of Perse in an unbroken phrase, including all facets of existence, creates and orders a world of extraordinary dimensions.

By means of his intellect, Perse identified the origin of his universe with the nebulous yet violent breath swirling in interplanetary space and in the abysses of time. The creative breath, the life-giving "souffle" has its closest counterpart in the searching wind. It is the wind which he interrogates as he stands on the threshold of a new world: "Levant un doigt de chair dans la ruée du vent, j'interroge, Puissance! Et toi, fais attention que ma demande n'est pas usuelle. / Car l'exigence en nous fut grande . . . / Et mon visage encore est dans le vent" (II, 46). It is with a torch and a flame in the wind that all men must seek clarification (II, 81), because by its devastations it provokes great works of the spirit. It searches out the weaknesses of men, it sweeps away the detritus of the past, it destroys the disorders of the soul, it disperses the ephemeral and the transient, and it clears the face of the earth and reveals the source of things to come.

Perse's spirit is that of the questing wind on all of the "pistes" of the globe. In his search for origin and meaning, he is an adventurer of the soul, transfixed by the fury of the elements, bewildered by universal disorder, assailed by the god. When understanding comes, it is sudden and he witnesses the unfolding of a new world: "Et la maturation, soudain, d'un autre monde au plein midi de notre nuit" (II, 83). The new world perceived is re-created by the poet among us in the poem which gives a promise for the future. Inspired by the divine fire immanent in the elements, the poet must interpret the message perceived by his intellect, his senses, and his sensibility. The mission of poets to mankind is an imperative. They must serve as "l'épine à votre chair; la pointe même au glaive de l'esprit. L'abeille du langage est sur leur front, / Et sur la lourde phrase humaine, pétrie de tant d'idiomes, ils sont seuls à manier la fronde de l'accent" (II, 105).

The universe of Perse is engendered not only by the destructive violence of the wind, but also by the creative movement of the sea. The origin and nature of the universe are virtually one and the same. The nature of the sea is that of the entire created universe and that of the spiritual universe as well: unfathomable, immense and immeasurable, opulent, eruptive, agitated, disordered, yet vivifying. As such it is glorified by the poet in *Amers*. In a letter to Roger Caillois, Perse rejects the idea proffered by some of his critics that his poetry is a crystallization, because for him, poetry is movement. Hence, the importance of the sea for the poet.[1] The sea, as actuality and symbol, is present in all of Perse's works from *Eloges* to *Oiseaux*. The ceaseless motion of its broad expanse symbolizes the continuous process of creation and existence. Its constant and creative movement is important to Perse who regards immobility as stagnant and non-creative. Despite the cyclical upheavals of civilizations, he expresses optimism because upheavals indicate evolution and growth. He considers inertia as a threat to growth: "L'inertie seule est menaçante." In *Poésie*, he speaks of the continuous flux of Being which changes the form and measure of all things: "Mais rien non plus ne garde forme ni mesure, sous l'incessant afflux de l'Etre" (pp. 17–18). Perse thus echoes Claudel who in *Art Poétique* had already described the effect of movement and vibration on the form and rhythm of all objects. For both poets then, movement is the principle of existence, the characteristic of every created thing.

Perse's poems are movement: animated, violent, fecund, rhythmic. The universe which they portray is all movement: armies on the march, migrations of peoples, evolutions of mankind and of cultures, physical and spiritual agitation of individuals, the turbulence and violence of nature; and the soul of the poet is in eruption as he is stirred by the breath and fire of creation. It is this evidence of total movement that gives a unifying tone to the poems of Perse.

Another constant in the universe of Perse is that of splendor. The world is transfigured in the mind of the poet. Glory, beauty, and joy pervade, enfold and transcend all turmoil, violence and chaos. Splendor is implied in the cyclical resurgence and rebirth which inevitably follow the devastation and destruction. In the last strophe of *Vents*, an epic of violence, one reads:

1. *La Poétique de Saint-John Perse* (Paris, 1954), pp. 180–81.

> Quand la violence eut renouvelé le lit des hommes sur la terre,
> Un très vieil arbre, à sec de feuilles, reprit le fil de ses maximes...
> Et un autre arbre de haut rang montait déjà des grandes Indes souterraines,
> Avec sa feuille magnétique et son chargement de fruits nouveaux. (II, 121)

Splendor in the universe and in created beings becomes even more luminous when contrasted with or revealed within a repulsive setting. It would seem that the existence of the ugly and imperfect is as necessary for the perception of beauty as the presence of evil is for an awareness of the presence of good. Consider the poet speaking of the spirit of God being reflected in the split liver of the eagle: "Jadis, l'esprit du dieu se reflétait dans les foies d'aigles entr'ouverts . . ." (II, 15); and in the same strophe, divinity illuminating the dawn of the living: ". . . et la divinité de toutes parts assiégeait l'aube des vivants."

Perse seems always to discern the seat of origin of the creative force itself in places of material or intellectual discord. Yet, in the midst of the worst disorders of the spirit, there is created a new style of grandeur as the setting for future acts. The genius of the poet, in moments of doubt, seems infested with the odor of dead forges. Soon, however, he becomes aware that the creative gods are assembling: "Les dieux s'assemblent sur les sources / Et c'est murmure encore de prodiges parmi les hautes narrations du large" (II, 36). And the poet is drawn westward by the splendor of the sky and the freshness of virgin lands stretching beneath the shadows. The splendor of the West reveals itself in the nubile and vigorous earth, in the foliage of its magnificent trees, and in the freshness of its free-flowing waters:

> . . . Des terres neuves, par là-bas, dans un très haut parfum d'humus et de feuillages,
> Des terres neuves, par là-bas, sous l'allongement des ombres les plus vastes de ce monde, . . .
> . . . Des terres neuves, par là-haut, comme un parfum puissant de grandes femmes mûrissantes . . .
> Toute la terre aux arbres, par là-haut, dans le balancement de ses plus beaux ombrages, ouvrant sa tresse la plus noire

et l'ornement grandiose de sa plume, comme un parfum de
chair nubile et forte au lit des plus beaux êtres de ce monde.
(*Vents*, II, 39–40)

The splendor of the natural world is only one aspect of the
glory of Perse's universe. It engenders and interacts with the
splendor of the human spirit. The saga of man's journey, para-
phrased in *Anabase* and in other poems, is majestic in the depic-
tion of his confrontation with nature, with the problems of
existence, and with himself. Man seems to have the will to
continue, to extend himself. In his push toward new frontiers,
in his movement toward new epochs, there is the spirit of the
explorer and the conqueror. Over the ages does this spirit mani-
fest itself repeatedly as it encounters the unknown and the
unexplored: "Et c'est une fraîcheur d'eaux libres et d'ombrages,
pour la montée des hommes de tout âge . . ." (II, 40).

The promise of the future and the freshness of new lands
present a challenge and an invitation. What wonders can the
human spirit accomplish in the new lands? Of what does man
dream as he reads the signs of things to come? Great are the
conquests to be realized in the open spaces: "Et c'est naissance
encore de prodiges sur la terre des hommes" (II, 41). The splen-
dor of the human spirit manifests itself in its ability to withstand
the ravages of the natural elements and overcome the obstacles
of sea, mountain, and desert. It is these very obstacles which sift
out the fear, the weakness, and the doubt. It is the wind which
Perse salutes as keeping the soul free of doubt:

> Eâ, dieu de l'abîme, les tentations du doute seraient
> promptes
> Où vient à défaillir le Vent . . . Mais la brûlure de l'âme
> est la plus forte,
> Et contre les sollicitations du doute, les exactions de l'âme
> sur la chair
> Nous tiennent hors d'haleine, et l'aile du Vent soit avec
> nous! (II, 34)

And so man stands "de ce côte du Siècle" ready to move into
the future.

Those who, in Perse's chronicle, moved forward to fulfill the
dream and the longings of the spirit were seeking, each accord-
ing to a personal imperative, to satisfy a material or a psycholog-

ical necessity. Despite the goal, theirs was a manifestation of the tenacity of the human spirit. These were the adventurers who cultivated the land, built the cities, founded the new religions, and began a civilization.

Another facet of the human spirit is the splendor of the intellect. The poet, pursuing his high mission, symbolizes this quality: ". . . c'est à l'imagination poétique que s'allume encore la haute passion des peuples en quête de clarté" (*Poésie*, p. 15). In his exploration of the dimensions and the mystery of human existence, the poet penetrates the dark and obscure corners of the universe. Unlike the builders, the reformers, and the seekers of wealth, the poet is an "adventurer of the soul" seeking the principle of being: "Car notre quête n'est plus de cuivres ni d'or vierge, n'est plus de houilles ni de naphtes, mais comme aux bouges de la vie le germe même sous sa crosse, et comme aux antres du Voyant le timbre même sous l'éclair, nous cherchons, dans l'amande et l'ovule et le noyau d'espèces nouvelles, au foyer de la force l'étincelle même de son cri!" (II, 73). How does the intellect go beyond the barriers of the seeds of being? By what method can the mind penetrate the infinite universe of the kernel, the ovule, or the nucleus to discover their inception? The poet encounters a cipher, yielding nothing. His attempts at deciphering assume the nebulosity of a vision, and it is this which he transcribes into reality. Even this effort seems to be in vain, and doubt and a schism of the spirit prevail. Splendor is evident, nevertheless, in the effort and the dimensions of the imagination. The poet stands watch for "l'irruption du dieu nouveau."

During the impasse, invective is hurled at matter, resplendent in its shrine of shadows and silence. This attitude gives way to an expressed belief in a future revelation: "Tu te révéleras! chiffre nouveau: dans les diagrammes de la pierre et les indices de l'atome; / Aux grandes tables interdites où plus fugaces vont les signes . . ." (II, 76).

The poet is not the sole "aventurier de l'âme." The man of science also attempts to penetrate the labyrinth of knowledge. Both are seeking answers: "Car l'interrogation est la même qu'ils tiennent sur un même abîme . . ." (*Poésie*, 13). Both poet and savant are confronted by the same mystery; and the scientist must often supplement his logic with intuition.

Man, the splendor of Creation, supersedes, therefore, inanimate matter in the poet's inventory of the universe: "car c'est de l'homme qu'il s'agit, dans sa présence humaine . . ." (II, 77). This refrain is often repeated, revealing Perse's concern. He speaks for men of all conditions, men from the depths and from the heights. As the interrogators of the sea, the sky, and the expanse of the universe seek answers to an apparent confusion, he, the poet, desires that they be melded and consumed by a flame for greater understanding. In the same manner that lightning sets the aphasiac on the path of "songes véridiques" so might there be born in the mind of man a new and ordered world.

The wish of the poet for man is one of fulfillment. In his interrogation, he must not become embittered by a taste of nothingness—"Et les capsules encore du néant dans notre bouche de vivants" (II, 91). Haunted though he may be by the eternal presence of death, man must embrace life to its limits: "Si vivre est tel, qu'on s'en saisisse! Ah! qu'on en pousse à sa limite, / D'une seule et même traite dans le vent, d'une seule et même vague sur sa course, / Le mouvement!" (*Vents*, II, 92). Thus Perse seems to negate the existentialist posture of the absurdity and meaninglessness of life because of the certainty of death. Life offers fulfillment in love, laughter, and adventure. It is in the flesh of women that the interrogators must rediscover the zest of life and the ecstasy of being. The adventurer, as he moves westward, his course sprinkled with joy and small triumphs, remembers:

> De grandes filles nous furent données, qui dans leurs bras d'épouses dénouaient plus d'hydres que nos fuites.
> Où êtes-vous qui étiez là, silencieux arome de nos nuits, ô chastes libérant sous vos chevelures impudiques une chaleureuse histoire de vivantes?
> Vous qui nous entendrez un soir au tournant de ces pages, sur les dernières jonchées d'orage, Fidèles aux yeux d'orfraies, vous saurez qu'avec vous
> Nous reprenions un soir la route des humains. (II, 93–94)

The promises of a new world in time and space are heightened by the fact that one leaves behind in memory the tedium of old ways, the horrors of war, the false security of prudence, the embarrassments of humility, the weakness of clandestine love, the debris of a tired epoch, and frustrations due to the limitations of reason. "Qu'on nous débonde tout cela! Qu'on nous divise ce pain d'ordure et de mucus. Et tout ce sédiment des âges sur leur phlegme!" (II, 113). The rush westward and seaward leads to a freshness of new experiences, "Un monde à naître sous vos pas! hors de coutume et de saison!" (II, 115). There in a new year and a new world, the soul takes possession of a new estate. In his promise to man, the poet indicates that the future lies at the end of a straight line, and not on a curve which leads back to a decadent past. It is a future as limitless in time as the universe is in space. The cycle of creation and destruction or dissolution is eternal. The debris of a worn-out existence may be blown away by the wind or washed away by the waters, but the seed of that existence, the principle of being remains constant and its source of origin unknown.

It is the ceaseless search for this ineffable source which maintains the luminosity of man's intellect and testifies to the intensity of his desire to know. Joy comes from the quest and the adventure.

That which is perceived by the senses forms the contours and fills the immensity of Perse's universe. Another dimension to his conception of the cosmos is formed by intuition and perceived intellectually. He seems to concur with pre-Socratic philosophers in some of their ideas on first principles and the nature of Being. Some reflection of his study of Empedocles is evident in his concept of the sense-perceived plurality of reality within the unity of the universe, and the elements of this plurality as the first principles of Being. To the elements earth, air, fire, and water, Empedocles adds Love and Strife, which, according to this physical philosopher, set the other elements in motion. This movement results in unity or separation. Symbolically, Perse's physical universe is structured on the violence of the elemental forces. He polarizes his moral universe on Love and Strife. Love is the unifying force, while Strife is disruptive in its manifestations and in its effects. Both bring about a re-ordering of the pattern. Strife, because of its nature, seems to characterize the universe in human relations. In the continuing cycle, however, Love is the restorative force.

In the poetry of Perse, strife takes many forms and Love has many faces. In enumerating and describing events, epochs, and cultures, Perse alludes to a prevailing discordance. The cataclysms of nature result in destruction, and similarly, human conflict causes chaos. He describes conflicts between conqueror and conquered, races, nations, and the culture and customs of their peoples. These allusions to relations among men and nations encompass actions, attitudes, beliefs, and practices which because of their nature, tend to end in strife or violence. The poetry of Perse is laudatory of man in his splendor, but it does not fail to catalogue man in his perfidy, in his enmity, in his injustice, in his cruelty, in his bigotry, and in all aspects of weakness and villainy. Perse is concerned with "le monde entier des choses."

The winds reveal "l'usure et la sécheresse au coeur des hommes investis . . ." (II, 12). They are invoked to sweep away "tout ce leurre! Sécheresse et supercherie d'autels . . ." (II, 22). The decadent city is illuminated by flashes of lightning as "un golgotha d'ordure et de ferraille" (II, 30). "Basse époque, sous l'éclair, que celle qui s'éteint là!" (II, 31). On the westward march, there are observed the vestiges of war: broken lances, whitened bones and the carcasses of animals. As the Poet turns southward, he observes the symbols of decay resulting from internecine strife and bigotry (II, 48–57). Perhaps the wind will carry it all away.

The greed of man is represented by those who on the westward march were seeking only wealth and land-titles: "Mais leur enquête ne fut que de richesses et de titres . . . Les buses sur les cols, prises aux courbes de leur vol, élargissaient le cirque et la mesure de l'avoir humain" (II, 70). Also among the migrants were barterers and businessmen, men of the law and men of the Church who would be guilty of abuse and self-aggrandizement:

Et puis vinrent les hommes, d'échange et de négoce. Les hommes de grands parcours gantés de buffle pour l'abus. Et tous les hommes de justice, assembleurs de police et leveurs de milice. Les Gouverneurs en violet prune avec leurs filles de chair rousse au parfum de furet.

Et puis les gens de Papauté en quête de grands Vicariats; les Chapelains en selle et qui rêvaient, le soir venu, de beaux diocèses jaune paille aux hémicycles de pierre rose . . . (II, 70, 71)

In his song of man in exile, man on the march, man confronted with "l'horreur de vivre" and "l'honneur de vivre," the poet envisages a future for humanity in which a great force will wipe out discord and disunity. In describing men refreshed by the storm and entering a new epoch, Perse paraphrases the prophet Micah who predicted that men would beat their swords into ploughshares and their spears into pruning hooks. He sees arising on new shores a race of new men united by love: "Et vous pouvez remettre au feu les grandes lames couleur de foie sous l'huile. Nous en ferons fers de labour, nous connaîtrons encore la terre ouverte pour l'amour, la terre mouvante, sous l'amour, d'un mouvement plus grave que la poix . . . (II, 119). Une race nouvelle parmi les hommes de ma race, une race nouvelle parmi les filles de ma race" (II, 120).

As others before him, particularly Empedocles, Perse draws an analogy between cosmic and human love. In *Amers*, he details the nature of the sea—that microcosmic replication of the universe. Pluralistic yet unified, chaotic yet ordered, convulsive yet quiescent, the sea is the matrix of being, the procreating substance. The four elements which make up the cosmos according to ancient philosophers are considered by Perse as forming the tetrarchy of the universe. Of these four, it is water which claims the attention of the poet. With the poem he will honor the ocean as it raises its "tête de Tétrarque." Such a song of the sea he will sing as has never been sung before. The sea within the poet, infusing him with its wisdom and joy to the point of satiety, will create the ode. For years, the poem had gestated in his spirit as a delicate thing to be nourished until it could spring forth full-blown, "Car il y avait un si longtemps que j'avais goût de ce poème . . ." (*Amers*, 138). In the midst of small talk in far-off places, his thoughts would swing back to Guadeloupe, "le beau pays natal," and to the broad expanses of the sea. The poem itself is a sensual experience for the poet. The sense of the ode is that of a nuptial song, a votive offering to the beloved. Both the tone and theme of *Amers* reflect voluptuousness. All of the symbols, images, allusions, and the direct language of love are present. In spite of the formal and ceremonious framework, befitting as it does a nuptial occasion, the poem reaches its climax in the highly sensual evocation of the marital consummation of conjugal love. The poem, the sea, and woman—are they separate and distinct entities in the mind of the poet? It is impossible to know. The suggestion is strong, however, that they are one and the same.

Always for Perse the sea is a woman, who is both the Aphrodite of cosmic love, and the Aphrodite Pandemos of earthly love. Though engendered in the sea-foam, she is probably sister to the very human and languorous Aphrodite of Praxiteles rather than to the formal and idealistic Venus of Botticelli. In the love-duet, the lover tells his mate: ". . . tu n'es point Vierge des grands fonds, Victoire de bronze ou de pierre blanche que l'on ramène, avec l'amphore . . ." (II, 228). An issue of the sea, hers is a woman's body born of a woman (II, 254).

The title "Etroits sont les vaisseaux" of *Amers* furnishes the motif for the setting, the physical attributes of the lovers, their sentiment, and the act of love. The breadth of the empire of love in time and space is compared to the expanse of the seas whose waves continue to bring through the ages, from remote times and distant spaces, the same promise of love as in the days of Helen of Troy. The same wave of love "rolls its haunches" toward the lovers who pay homage to the sea in its alliance with love. They exult because of the truth of love, the divine vivacity of love, the divine diversity of creation—male and female. The narrowness of the female body is compared to that of a sleek vessel, resembling as it does its build of nacelle, hull, curves of the keel, yielding timbers, and median opening. She bears the signs of a summer sea with its warmth and radiance. Her skin of lacquered gold is veiled in its own radiance; her flesh, her hair, the nape of the neck, even the arm-pits seem to be scorched by love and afire with the fever of love. She is like the sands of the shore in warmth and odor; she also has the smell of green water and reefs, seaweed and copper. Her taste is that of the seed and sap of sweetness, acid mingled with milk, salt with blood, gold with iodine, the savor of copper, all the sea as in the maternal urn. Her body bears the divine signature and the ritual incision heightened by a red stroke. The lover addresses her: "Tu es l'idole de cuivre vierge, en forme de poisson, que l'on enduit au miel de roche ou de falaise . . . Tu es la mer elle-même dans son lustre, lorsque midi, ruptile et fort, renverse l'huile de ses lampes" (II, 236). Even more figuratively, she to him is the promise of the Orient, the approach of dawn, the premonition of the dream, the invisible itself at the source of its emission, the invisible essence of the flame.

The love-song continues as the woman compares the musculature of her lover's loins to the rippling of the waters, and the copper odor of his male body to that of the sea. "L'Amante" feels that on his lips she is keener than thirst and wants him to be refreshed at the spring of her body. And so she unfolds on the sea of love as did the wave that engendered her, and her body opens as shamelessly to "l'Etalon du sacre" as the sea to strokes of lightning. To him she says, "La nuit t'ouvre une femme: son corps, ses havres, son rivage; et sa nuit antérieure où gît toute mémoire" (II, 232). It is license that she desires for the play of the body as her hands range along the harness of his muscles. She compares him to the master of a ship who governs and directs her movement which is like that of marsh grass and the migration of sand toward the sea. In her mouth, his tongue is as the wildness of the sea with its taste of copper. He himself is the sea lingering on the shore of woman. In the dark recesses and along the curves of her body, he seeks the occult figure of her origin. The beating of their blood is that of the storms and of the high seas. In the words of the woman, the encounter continues as though it were a battle between adversaries:

Mais langue à langue, et souffle à souffle, haletante! la face
ruisselante et l'oeil rongé d'acide, celle qui soutient seule
l'ardente controverse, l'Amante hérissée, et qui recule et
s'arque et qui fait front, émet son sifflement d'amante et de
prêtresse . . .
Frapperas-tu, hampe divine?
. . . .
Tu frapperas, promesse! . . . Parle plus haut, despote! et
plus assidûment m'assaille: l'irritation est à son comble! Quête
plus loin, Congre royal: ainsi l'éclair en mer cherche la gaine
du navire . . .
Tu as frappé, foudre divine!—Qui pousse en moi ce très
grand cri de femme non sevrée? . . . Ô splendeur! ô tristesse!
et très haut peigne d'Immortelle coiffant l'écume radieuse!
et tout ce comble, et qui s'écroule, herse d'or! . . . J'ai cru
hanter la fable même et l'interdit. (II, 240–41)

And the lover embraces the woman as though she were a *mêlée*
of stars, and the soul is narrowly confined at the incision of the
body. Such is the language of the poet as he blends the sea, the
female, and the poem in his hymn to the joys of the flesh: "Une
même vague par le monde, une même vague notre course . . .
Etroite la mesure, étroite la césure, qui rompt en son milieu le
corps de femme comme le mètre antique . . ." (II, 238). There
is, according to Perse, no higher action, no higher usurpation,
no greater security, than can be found in the vessel of love.

Physical love gives an instant respite from the specter of
death, though it is itself a kind of death. Lovers hear the cicada
cry of death (II, 241). It is a sort of voluptuous shield against
nothingness and the inevitable destruction. Lovers combine their
forces against the monster "à tête biseautée." Thus they are
granted a reprieve from death; heart and body are freed in the
triumph of love. Love is an offense to death because it confers a
newness to life and a freshness of being. According to the poet,
the soul is renewed in the consummation of love. As a spur to
the soul, it revivifies spiritual man. He ceases to be earthbound
by the temporal. The absence and alienation reflected in his
eyes, the solitude of his heart, the nausea and boredom behind
the painted mask are shadows of the soul which can be cleared
away by divine immersion in the sea of love. "Et la femme est
dans l'homme, et dans l'homme est la mer, et l'amour loin de

mort sur toute mer navigue" (II, 269). The odor of woman is that of living things and the smile of living is in the breath of man; together they inhabit the reality of the dream. At the high noon of his being and free from his shadow, man salutes the purifying sea: "Et toi, tu nous assisteras contre la nuit des hommes . . . / Nous franchissons enfin le vert royal du Seuil; et faisant plus que te rêver, nous te foulons, fable divine!" (II, 290).

Using as he does, the real and the imaginary to attain a higher form of reality, according to Charpier,[2] Perse pre-figures another level of experience. This is made possible by the representational depiction of the force, beauty, and movement of the sea which suggests the spirit and its inner activity. The long double metaphor of the sea as a woman and as a universe, that is *Amers*, is extended in all directions. It centers however on the power, manifestations, and analogous nature of cosmic love with that of carnal love. The poem—words structured into invocation, strophe, choir, and dedication—implifies a confrontation of mind and matter and the domination of things by the spirit. This is indeed the most significant plateau of symbolization. Fourteen years after *Vents*, Perse pointed out in *Amers* the landmarks which lead to fulfillment in a world enveloped in harmony. *Vents* reveals the ugliness and decadence of the West; *Amers* catalogs those of the world. Ceremoniously do the processions of the ages make their way seaward for their lustration. Man finds himself caught in a morass created by greed and technology and fear. The needs of the spirit are neglected. He realizes that the confines of the earth are too limiting, and preoccupation with the tangible too blinding for the expression of love: "En vain la terre proche nous trace sa frontière" (II, 224). Therefore he must move toward the shore, toward the conciliating sea, forsaking the restraints of the land—"l'antique Magicienne: la terre et ses glands fauves, la lourde tresse circéenne..." (II, 157–58).

Immersion in divine waters laves man of his stains, his ugliness, and his vain attachments. Emotions of joy, grace, and love are quickened by the turbulence and he experiences the joy of being

2. Jacques Charpier, *Saint-John Perse* (Paris, 1962), p. 98.

which is a joy of the spirit. Liberated by the act of purification, man rediscovers the primordial essense of innocence, buried and forgotten beneath layers of civilization. He knows that he is alive; he knows that he co-exists with a world of beings in limitless time and space; he knows that harmonious co-existence is only possible in a world suffused with love. This is the great cosmic force which gives order to a disordered world. Thus does the poet fulfill his mission. He restores man's spirit and reconciles him with a chaotic universe by disclosing an ordered pattern and purpose beneath the disorder: "ô mémoire, au coeur d'homme, du royaume perdu!" (II, 340).

Great cavalcades of past civilizations, their peoples and their legends flood the poet's mind: ". . . une foule en hâte se levant aux travées de l'Histoire et se portant en masse vers l'arène, dans le premier frisson du soir au parfum de fucus, / Récitation en marche vers l'auteur et vers la blanche peinte de son masque" (II, 141). All of the debris of history is cast into oblivion in the vast chasm of splendor which is the sea (II, 275–76). But what of the future? Is this the end? It is from the sea that the poet receives a promise for the future: "La Mer, en nous, portant son bruit soyeux du large et toute sa grande fraîcheur d'aubaine par le monde" (II, 133). From the sea arises a new splendor and the world renews its foundations (II, 276).

VI. Re-Creation
of the Universe—Claudel

The creative force of the universe is not a nameless entity for Claudel. His concept of the origin of the universe is that recounted in Genesis—from the breath of God into the void to that which he breathed to create man, the summit of his handiwork. In "La Légende de Prakriti," Claudel explains the term "créer" as making something from nothing. It is God who originated the first idea and its image. He constructed being and set it in motion: "Il a tout fait. Il a tout créé. Mail Il a tout fait dans l'ordre et dans la charité, Se servant de ce qui était avant pour amener ce qui est après, utilisant à mesure les moyens qu'Il s'est procurés, et parmi eux cette spontanéité, cette aptitude inventive, productrice et reproductrice de la nature, la réponse de cette cavité qu'Il a gonflée de Son souffle."[1] In the order of creation, God made land and water, informed them of his requirements, furnished the force and matter, and

1. *Figures et Paraboles* (Paris, 1936), p. 152–53.

directed them in the construction of their instruments. In man, He insufflated a spirit, a soul, and an intelligent and autonomous principle. These qualities enable man to see within himself and comprehend that which was created: "Dieu en nous donnant la conscience, nous a ouvert un oeil non seulement sur le fond de nous-mêmes, mais sur toutes les forces intérieures de production et de développement de ce monde qu'Il a fait. Nous n'avons qu'à regarder en nous-mêmes pour y trouver disposés la Terre, la Mer, le Ciel étoile. . . ."[2] Claudel thus believes that the material macrocosm of the universe is implanted in the immaterial microcosm that is the soul of man. Such an unquestioning faith! This God-given insight and intuitiveness, recognized by Claudel and questioned by Perse, made it possible nevertheless for both poets to comprehend and express the nature of the created world.

For both writers, the world is movement and vibration. Claudel presents this idea in *Art Poétique* and in subsequent works. The idea of movement is presented in his discourse on time and space. Movement derives from the fact of two different bodies existing in space. It is a property of every created thing, and the form of each thing is determined by the external force exerted on it by other things. "Pas une chose qui ne soit nécessaire aux autres" (V, 282). Each object then is dependent and forms a part of an indivisible whole. Just as each word in a composition gives meaning to every other word in the uniform movement of the writing process, so do created objects, as the innumerable transcription of a pure celestial movement give meaning to each other. In comparing the universe as a time-making machine to the mechanism of a clock, Claudel defines movement as displacement resulting from a force outside of the body displaced. The displaced body has a tendency to return to its original place. The design traced by the movement of the body in space indicates time (*Art Poétique*, 135–38). Just as objects vibrate in contact with other objects, so does matter vibrate in contact with a different reality, the Spirit.

There is movement from without and movement within an object. The imprisoned movement within a body causes vibration. Vibration then is a constant quality of matter and an essen-

2. Ibid., p. 110.

tial of human life; it makes existence possible. Pierre Angers in his interpretation of *Art Poétique* writes of the creature which at each moment passes from nothingness to being under the uninterrupted impulsion of the First Cause: "The creature, at each instant, in a radical dependence, receives from God the privilege of existing; it persists, thanks to a gift unceasingly renewed, in a state of perpetual birth: its being traces a course in duration; it is the track of a continuous mobility."[3] The vibration and movement of the individual thing or being are also those of the universe, due similarly to the First Cause.

Claudel makes an analogy between the movement of the physical world and that of the soul which in its "frémissement" seeks to reunite itself with the Source. While Perse regards the turbulence of the physical world as the Source itself, Claudel considers such turbulence as manifestations of divine will. The impact of the meaning of reality on both poets differs because of their personal teleological concepts. Claudel supports the argument of a Providence-directed purpose and the interdependence of the world. He therefore molds and projects a poetic universe grounded in his personal belief of divine truth and revelation.

Claudel utilizes the sea as a major symbol because its continuous movement and the mobility of that which lies beneath its surface parallel the universe. It is an interdependent unity made up of a myriad of disparate components. Such aspects create for the poet insight into a limitless, unseen cosmos. In an early trip across the Indian Ocean, Claudel sensed the purity revealed by the brilliance of the sun reflected in the mirror of the becalmed sea. It was to him a revelation of the ineffable essense of the Infinite—formless, colorless, pure, absolute, fulminant, made momentarily visible during its unyielding struggle against evil *(Partage de Midi*, I, 914).[4] The illuminating and searing sun which evoked the image may be compared to Picasso's disinterested eye of God in the *Guernica.* As Claudel's God, however, He would be concerned with the human condition and

3. *Commentaire à l'Art Poétique de Paul Claudel* (Paris, 1949), p. 25.
4. *Théâtre*, 2 vols. (Paris, 1947–48). All references from *Partage de Midi* and *Le Soulier de Satin* are from this edition.

with affording man a fleeting glimpse of divinity. In "L'Esprit et l'Eau," Claudel acknowledges this "minute de lumière à voir" (II, 244). As Mésa in *Partage de Midi*, he speaks of the effect of this sudden revelation on his senses. He seems disembodied and in communication with the past and the future. He is Rimbaud's "voyant" caught up in a trance of mystic awareness: "Le rapt sec." It is in this divorced state of the poet from the mundane present that the poem itself engenders and is engendered.

Mésa wishes to understand things as they really are! He feels as though he were newly-created man standing between the waters and the sky at the dawn of creation. The feeling of disorientation and alienation when confronted by "le néant" and the profound silence conjointly release in the poet a creative energy and establish a bond between himself and the Creator. In "L'Esprit et l'Eau," the poet as co-creator writes: "Voici l'Ode, voici que cette grande Ode nouvelle vous est présente, / Non point comme une chose qui commence, mais peu à peu comme la mer qui était là, / La mer de toutes les paroles humaines . . ." (II, 235). Then addressing the Creator: "Dieu qui avez soufflé sur le chaos . . . / Vous commandez de même à mes eaux, vous avez mis dans mes narines le même esprit de création et de figure" (II, 243). This affirmation of the liaison had already been expressed by Mésa: "Il vit, je vis; il pense et je pèse en mon coeur sa pensée. / Lui qui a fait mes yeux, est-ce que je puis ne point le voir? lui-même qui a fait mon coeur" (*Partage*, I, 931). This oneness would enable him to fulfill the desire he had before his flight to China: "Moi qui aimais tellement ces choses visibles, ô j'aurais voulu voir, avoir avec appropriation, / Non point avec les yeux seulement, ou les sens seulement, mais avec l'intelligence de l'esprit, / Et tout connaître afin d'être tout connu" (*Partage*, I, 931). The poet subjects his total self to the task of deciphering. Contact with the concrete informs the physical self and illuminates the spirit. It is the knowledge and the experience of this uninterrupted, vibratory contact which enable Claudel to delineate the illusive sense of things.

Movement as a characteristic of the universe is not random movement. It is rhythmic and unending motion. A flaw in the rhythm or an interruption would destroy the harmony of the created world and disrupt the re-creative pattern of the universe. "Il y a une harmonie, à chaque temps de la durée entre toutes les parties de la création, depuis le Séraphin jusqu'au ver" (*Art Poétique*, 202). Each object intermeshes with every other object in realizing the final cause. Witness the rhythm of the seasons, the tides of the oceans, the movement of the planets, the cycle of night and day and life and death in this closed and finite universe. The brief and spasmodic upheavals of nature such as earthquakes, hurricanes, and cyclones have no effect on the rhythm and harmony of the creative movement, mighty though they be in their manifestation. The extent of such upheavals is equated with Mésa's passion for Ysé:

> Et je te sens sous moi passionnément qui abjure, et en moi le profond dérangement
> De la création, comme la Terre
> Lorsque l'écume aux lèvres elle produisait la chose aride, et que dans un rétrécissement effroyable
> Elle faisait sortir sa substance et le repli des monts comme de la pâte! (*Partage*, I, 957)

These occurrences, as a part of the plan, serve to erase that which is disharmonious in time and space: "Et la neige sur elle descend comme une absolution" (III, 256). This is also a theme of Saint-John Perse.

The balanced movement of the universe is multiple and redundant. Each particle of creation is a universe in itself, balanced, mobile, and re-creative. In *La Cantate à trois voix*, Laeta speaks of a rose: ". . . Du monde entier en cette fleur suprême éclose!" (*Oeuvre Poétique*, 334). Unseen and unknown, propulsion is provided from an inexhaustible source. Therein lies the mystery of the eternal. The continuity of the eternal whose beginning and end are beyond knowledge and whose renewal is inexhaustible reflects the character of the universe: "Il ne cesse point continuité, non plus que de l'âme au corps" (II, 241). Claudel viewed "l'inexhaustible cérémonie vivante," as a world to be invaded and explained in the limitless space of the poem (I, 231). The creative force of the poet is as great as that of the tree which each year creates new life:

Comme l'arbre au printemps nouveau chaque année
Invente, travaillé par son âme,
Le vert, le même qui est éternel, crée de rien sa feuille
pointue,
Moi, l'homme,
Je sais ce que je fais,
De la poussée et de ce pouvoir même de naissance et de
creation
J'use, je suis maître,
Je suis au monde, j'exerce de toutes parts ma connaissance.
Je connais toutes choses et toutes choses se connaissent en
moi.
J'apporte à toute chose so délivrance. (II, 238)

The inexhaustible ceremony of creation which repeats itself
within the smallest and the greatest also fixes an interdependent
bond of kinship. A spiritual essence flows from thing to thing
and maintains universal unity and continuity.

As an entity, the universe is complete, and so is each individual
thing within the cosmos. There is a sufficiency in the created
world which assures balance, harmony, renewal and continuity.
The completeness of the universe prevents anything from being
added or subtracted: "Nous avons conquis le monde et nous
avons trouvé que Votre Création est finie, / Et que l'imparfait
n'a point de place avec Vos oeuvres finies, et que notre imagi-
nation ne peut pas ajouter / Un seul chiffre à ce Nombre en
extase devant Votre Unité" (V, 289). This is the image Claudel
projects of a closed and indestructible universe in "La Maison
Fermée" in which he elaborates on the idea of God's will. In the
second ode he had said: "Il est fermé par votre volonté comme
par un mur et par votre puissance comme par une très forte
enceinte!" (II, 240). This image of a closed universe supports
the theme of completeness, continuity, coherence, and solidar-
ity. There are implications as to the meaning of the physical
and spiritual worlds, humanity and individual man, and the in-
visible bond which holds all together. The very idea of "closed"
suggests an interior activity with purpose.

The unity of the physical world foreshadows the unity of
mankind with God. Before this liaison can possibly be estab-
lished, mankind must achieve a collective and an individual

unity. Man must explore the abyss within himself and become aware of the emptiness and the barrier which stand between his being and God's grace. To fill the void and break down the barrier, whatever its nature, is the Catholic poet's duty. Claudel sees himself as the "être fini" in the image of God's perfection (V, 284) destined to reveal to man his insufficiency. The void in man exists when there is an absence of God. The poet hopes that "la parole juste" will be efficacious in re-establishing a bond broken since the dawn of creation. In order to find the exact word, he is willing to forage sea and sky and go to the ends of the earth (*La Messe là-bas*, 500).[5] As God's ambassador, he must reveal to mankind God's presence: "Ce Néant au bord duquel ils sont depuis si longtemps assis, ce Vide laissé par l'absence de l'Etre, où se joue le reflet du Ciel, il fallait leur apporter Dieu pour qu'ils le comprennent tout à fait" (*Soulier de Satin*, II, 727–28).

The feeling of exile which man experiences in his personal and closed universe may be a necessity so that he can "comprendre la patrie." (*La Cantate à trois voix*, 347). The effort to overcome the sense of isolation by secular pursuits is in vain. He suffers the "soif affreuse" of Rodrigue which can be satisfied only by the spirit. The Guardian Angel refers to the exploits of Don Rodrigue as being less a question of discovering a new world than that of finding again an old world which was lost. It is a nostalgic yearning for a lost paradise and for a restoration of the wholeness of being (*Soulier*, II, 726–28). Rodrigue explains to Daibutsu his purpose in exploring the world:

> C'est parce que je suis un homme catholique, c'est pour que toutes les parties de l'humanité soient réunies et qu'il n'y en ait aucune qui se croie le droit de vivre dans son hérésie,
> Séparée de toutes les autres comme si elles n'en avaient pas besoin.
>
> . . . .
>
> Vous ne serez plus seuls! Je vous apporte le monde, la parole totale de Dieu, tous ces frères qu'ils vous plaisent ou non à apprendre bon gré mal gré, tous ces frères en un seul géniteur. (*Soulier*, II, 773)

5. *Oeuvre Poétique* (Paris, 1957). All references from *La Messe là-bas*, *La Cantate à trois voix*, and *Chemin de la Croix* are from this edition.

Claudel has a passion for mankind, all of whom are necessary to each other and to him. In order to restore a bond with God, a link must be forged to re-establish the solidarity of humanity. According to the poet, when each individual is born, there is established "un secret noeud" with his unknown fellowmen, those whom he will know and those whom he will not know, "ceux du prologue et ceux de l'acte dernier" (I, 228). He hopes to close any gap which may exist in the band of God's creatures (II, 239). He wants to invade the heart of man with a voice which is "La mesure sainte, libre, toute-puissante, créatrice!" (II, 247). Even though man's soul is closed to other men and to God, the Holy Spirit can unlock the door and join the imprisoned spirit of man, "l'esprit qui a fait la porte ouvre la serrure" (II, 237). The spirit of God seeks a habitation in the heart of man, suffused with "l'esprit immonde" of false gods and profane ideas. God's spirit can penetrate the closed circle of man's universe as water penetrates the earth. It establishes itself and purifies the soul and His presence is made manifest just as it is in the closed circle of the physical universe. This is a positive view of man's soul as a closed universe, filled with God's presence and immune to the invasion of evil. In the magnificent *Processionnal pour saluer le siècle nouveau*, Claudel presents the saints of the church and all mankind bound in catholic solidarity: "Voici l'immensité de tous mes frères vivants et morts, / l'unanimité du peuple catholique..." (*Oeuvre Poétique*, 300).

"Ce monde brut entier" with which the poet is concerned attests that God is principle, purpose, and presence "à qui tout consonne" (*La Messe*, 502). During his exploration of the world, Don Rodrigue is haunted by the word "why." Everything ponders the conditions of its existence:

> Pourquoi le vent sans fin qui me tourmente? dit le pin. A quoi est-ce qu'il est si nécessaire de se cramponner? Qu'est-ce qui meurt ainsi dans l'extase? dit le chrysanthème.
> —Qu'y a-t-il de si noir pour que j'existe, un cyprès?—Qu'est-ce qu'on appelle l'azur pour que je sois si bleu?—Qu'existe-t-il de si doux pour que je sois si rose?— ... —Que l'eau est une chose forte pour qu'elle m'ait valu ce coup de queue et cette jaquette d'écailles!—De quelle ruine, dit le rocher, suis-je le

décombre? A quelle inscription absente mon flanc est-il pré-
paré? (*Soulier*, II, 772)

Why the wind, death in ecstasy, blackness, the blue of the sky,
the sweetness of the rose, the scales of the fish, the crumbling
of the rock? Every act, movement, and condition is the gesture
of God. His purpose and presence are manifest in every state
of being in the physical world. The poet's intelligence responds
to this all-pervading presence: "Si le monde ne parlait tant de
Vous, mon ennui ne serait pas tel" (*La Messe*, 500). The whole
"octave de la Création" speaks of the immanence of God. Every-
thing is an expression of the Eternal and possesses some charac-
teristic or quality of the Creator. How does one describe the in-
effable nature of the Divine? The poet sees it in the purity of
the rose, the splendor of the sky, the freedom of water, the
energy of the sea, the harmonious movement of the planets, the
continuity of the seasons, the melody of music, the glory of
colors, the force of the storm, the abundance of harvests, the
passion of love, the joy of laughter, the oneness of mankind, the
efficacy of language, the eternity of time, the silence of dura-
tion, the infinity of space, the indestructibility of matter, and
the immortality of the soul.

And what of the imperfections, the disorder, the suffering,
evil, ugliness, human and natural catastrophes? How do they
relate to the Eternal? Nothing that God has made is vain; noth-
ing is foreign to our salvation (*Soulier*, II, 651). The antitheses
of being are necessary in that one term makes possible an aware-
ness of the other. The most common are good and evil, beauty
and ugliness, order and disorder, light and darkness, joy and
sorrow, being and non-being, love and hate, life and death.
Everything fits into the Plan. Doña Musique muses on the
purpose of God in the midst of great disorder:

> Qu'importe le désordre, et la douleur d'aujourd'hui puis-
> qu'elle est le commencement d'autre chose, puisque
> Demain existe, puisque la vie continue, cette démolition
> avec nous des immenses réserves de la création,
> Puisque la main de Dieu n'a pas cessé son mouvement qui
> écrit avec nous sur l'éternité en lignes courtes ou longues,

Jusqu'aux virgules, jusqu'au point le plus imperceptible,
Ce livre qui n'aura son sens que quand il sera fini.
. . . .
De tous ces mouvements épars je sais bien qu'il se prépare
un accord, puisque déjà ils sont assez unis pour discorder.
(*Soulier*, II, 691–92)

The chaotic movement of destruction becomes the harmonious movement of renewal.

Few concepts or experiences escape Claudel's consideration in the construct of his universe, since everything is made for a purpose: "Et moi je dis qu'il n'est rien dans la nature qui soit fait sans dessein et propos à l'homme adressé, / Et comme lumière pour l'oeil et le son pour l'oreille, ainsi toute chose pour l'analyse de l'intelligence . . ." (IV, 267). Thus he directs his intelligence to explore the universal themes of love and death. They are predominant in Claudelian thought and pervade all that he has written both in a real and symbolic sense. Both terms explain purpose and are involved in the scheme of salvation. Love, an imitation of the creative act of God, gives a glimpse of the ecstasy of eternal salvation and opens the door to it. Death leads one through the passage to immortality and salvation by re-uniting one's soul with God.

In his discussion of the implications of human love, Claudel's appraisal is not academic. His personal experience, recounted in the episodes of Mésa and Ysé and Rodriguez and Doña Prouhèze, reveals how human passion serves as an instrument of redemption. He had known the heights and depths of love. There are several stages from love to redemption in the relationship between man and woman, and for each stage there runs a parallel for divine love. Love is offered and sought, refused and accepted, sacrificed and betrayed. One suffers and one knows peace, experiences sorrow and joy, pain and pleasure, separation and unity.

It is the physical aspect of human love which Claudel most frequently equates with the divine. In *Soulier de Satin*, Doña Prouhèze, guilt-ridden and helpless in her love for Rodrigue, is concerned about her actions in the eyesight of God. She asks the Guardian Angel if God is jealous of lovers. The Angel asks if it is probable that God could be jealous of that which He created, and would He have made anything which did not serve Him. Prouhèze persists and replies that a man forgets God in the arms of a woman. To reassure her, the Angel asks how it is possible to forget God when one is with Him, and how can one be associated in the mystery of His creation except with Him. It is at this moment, he says, that one crosses for an instant into Eden through the gate of humiliation and death. Prouhèze then asks if love "hors du sacrement" is sinful. Even sin, the Angel says, serves the purpose of God.

Man in a state of isolation is unfulfilled and incomplete. The human soul in its abject condition of nothingness yearns for the consolation of another to fill the inexplicable void. Profane love as opposed to sacred love affords an immediate, if transient, solace. The obvious corollary is that divine love is eternal. Man's physical and metaphysical universe is indeed absurd if he stands in a vacuum and rejects the current of love which permeates the cosmos. Each inanimate object is one with the physical world. "Tout se tient." Each animate being must be one with each other. Man must become one with the world in order to achieve an initial unity of being. Otherwise, he is absent, circulating on the periphery of life as a soul lost in purgatory. In his dialogue with "la muse qui est la Grâce," an all-inclusive symbol of human love, divine love, and poetic inspiration, Claudel exclaims that he lacks unanimity unless he is one with the entire world around him (IV, 274). The affinity of mankind corresponds with the harmony of the universe; the affinity of man and woman establishes an inner harmony: "Et quelle chair pour parler à l'homme plus puissante que celle de la femme?" (*Soulier*, II, 723). In the "octave of Creation" man with woman thus becomes a harmonious chord. The discord of his spirit is nullified.

The beauty of woman serves as the magnet which attracts. In the presence of beauty, man experiences joy and satisfaction, harmony and peace. And so he seeks this simulation of divine grace to make him whole. Mésa explains to Ysé that he is made for joy as the bee for the heart of the flower. He expresses the profound discontent of man when he says that it is hard to be alone and unloved: "Il est dur de garder tout son coeur. Il est

dur de ne pas être aimé. Il est dur d'être seul. Il est dur d'atten-
dre, / Et d'endurer, et d'attendre, et d'attendre toujours . . ."
(*Partage*, I, 934). For Claudel, the effort to endure was like a
gnawing in the depths of his being or the torment of a secret
fire (I, 233).

Human love demands rupture and sacrifice. Mésa and Ysé
knew the total surrender of self to each other, and the total
alienation from all commitments, past and future. Theirs was
a rupture from responsibility, other relationships, and from
conscience. Similarly, the love of God demands absolute rup-
ture, alienation from the profane, sacrifice of the ephemeral
for the eternal. In *La Messe là-bas*, the poet warns that one can
only enter naked into the councils of love, divested of every-
thing profane (p. 501).

And what of consummation in conjugal love? The fire of
love welds and purifies; it establishes in man a sense of gratifica-
tion and tranquillity. Lorigiola speaks of this purifying flame
of love in his commentary on the *Odes*. Each man searches for
one who in a wild embrace will create with him a single great
flame. "Il suffire à ces deux êtres de se toucher pour que jaillisse
la grande flamme humaine."[6] In order to underscore the dimen-
sions of passion, Claudel translated the love duet of Eros and
Psyché by Patmore:

> Celui-ci:
> Sous votre sein, ma mortelle Aimante
> Immortelle par mon baiser, sens-tu
> L'élancement de cette peine exquise?
>
> . . . .
>
> Blâme le Dieu lui-même
> Si tout, autour de lui, éclate en flammes inextinguibles!
>
> . . . .
>
> O joie trop grande! ô toucher du feu subtil!
> O chaos de bonheur! ô désir imperturbable!
> Qui des fonds de l'esprit s'impartit à la cervelle et au sang.
> (*Oeuvre Poétique*, 313–18)[7]

6. "Les Grandes Odes de Claudel," *Les Etudes Classiques*, XXVII, no. 2
(April 1959), 166–67.
7. For the original version, see Coventry Patmore, *Poems: The Un-
known Eros* (London, 1879), IV, 160–72.

There is in the perfect physical union of man and woman the symbol of a closed circle, a filled void, the union of principle and purpose in the design of creation (IV, 273). Ysé speaks to the dying Mésa of their single life-giving love, clean and naked, "dans une interpénétration / Inexprimable, dans la volupté de la différence conjugale, l'homme et la femme comme deux grands animaux spirituels" (*Partage*, I, 987). This physical attachment of the creatures of God prefigures their attachment with God the Creator. In imitation of divine creation, the union produces a microcosm in the image and likeness of God. "Soyez béni," exults the poet-father, "parce que je ne demeure point unique, / Et que de moi il est sorti existence . . . et que de moi à mon tour, en cette image réelle pour jamais, d'une âme jointe avec un corps, / Vous avez reçu figure et dimension" (III, 258).

The flesh can be an instrument of redemption or a barrier to redemption. When it becomes a barrier, the rejection of its pleasures makes of it an instrument of grace. The sacrifice of self is an imitation of the sacrifice of Christ and a demonstration of supernal love. Thus it was with Prouhèze and Rodrigue. So great was their love it had to be rejected. Prouhèze was the cross of Rodrigue. On it he was crucified for their salvation:

> Si je ne puis être son paradis, du moins je puis être sa croix! Pour que son âme avec son corps y soit écartelée je vaux bien ces deux morceaux de bois qui se traversent!
> Puisque je ne puis lui donner le ciel, du moins je puis l'arracher à la terre. Moi seule puis lui fournir une insuffisance à la mesure de son désir!
>
> . . . .
> Il a demandé Dieu à une femme et elle était capable de le lui donner, car il n'y a rien au ciel et sur la terre que l'amour ne soit capable de donner! (*Soulier*, II, 681–82)

The question of sacrifice involves the choice exercised by man when he is confronted with salvation or damnation. Descartes's theory on the ability of the will to direct or control one's passions and desires has some merit. One's will, influenced by conscience or by the knowledge of the difference between good and evil, can direct one's actions toward the ultimate good. This will, translated into Claudelian theory, enables his characters to make the required sacrifice. Unlike the heroes of Corneille whose choice is between honor and personal satisfaction, Claudel's characters must make a choice for their salvation. If a man's choice is that of divine grace, he recognizes unequivocally that the sacrifice of personal or temporal bonds is his part. The very act of sacrifice implies a total unity of self, hence a unity with God.

A step toward unity of self is accomplished through an awareness of that which is internally eternal. Again, Descartes's "idée innée" of the presence of God, this intuition which establishes a tenuous link with the Creator. Claudel, too, believes that we are born with an inner knowledge of God. All that we know of the Eternal, according to him in the "Credo," "Il nous semble que nous l'avions toujours su . . ." (La Messe, 506). Finite, imperfect man, created by a perfect Being can scarcely ignore the existence of such a Being: "La fonction de tout être qui dans une autre volonté que la sienne se connaît créature, est de croire" ("Credo," La Messe, 505). Believing this, he yields himself completely "à la chose dont il a reçu naissance." The free and intuitive spirit of man ought to accept gratuitously the wonders of the physical world, Christ on the Cross, and all that which denies the "Néant" and affirms the "raison d'être" of mankind. Unity of self is further propelled by what Claudel calls the profound desire for good in us. He was explaining the dramatic structure of Soulier to Gide who had said that good sentiments do not create good literature. The poet retorted that it is less possible to write good literature with just bad sentiments than with just good ones. Moreover, the desire for good must be contoured with the passion for evil to avoid an insipid drama. Without the good or the desire for good, there is no evil. One term requires the other. Good presumes evil and vice versa. Both lead to struggle, without which there is no progress.[8] The spirit imbued with grace, through an innate knowledge of God, chooses the good and prepares itself for sacrifice.

It is only through the total integration of self that one is able to discern the shadows which cause him to be caught inextri-

8. "Le Soulier de Satin, version pour la scène. A propos de la première représentation du Soulier de Satin au Théâtre Français," Théâtre, II, 1307.

cably in a web of disaster. An inner awareness leads one to avoid such entanglements by seeking refuge in the eternal. Most shadows are masked and assume many forms. In his verbal struggle with the Muse who is Grace, Claudel lists the "ténèbres" which threaten to engulf him: those of intelligence, of sound, of the absence of God, and of his sinful heart (II, 245–46). Laeta admonishes the man whose priority is material not to put his lips to the chalice because that which nourishes the body does not satisfy the thirst of the soul (*Cantate*, 345). Fausta seeks to keep intact "la porte fatale" of her flesh from which there would be no return. She is willing to put aside her happiness and that of her husband for the good of the fatherland.

Sacrifice and renunciation of temporal and transient satisfaction entail sorrow, pain, and suffering. Are not these landmarks on the hidden path to God? Is not the one who suffers in Christ's name thus following the way of the Cross? This is one of the age-old explanations of why the good must suffer. "La souffrance, c'est à nous!" (*La Messe*, 503). Man is doomed to suffer because of original sin. This phase of man's existence on earth is what Ballanche calls "l'Epreuve," which is followed by "la Réhabilitation" and finally "l'Affranchissement" by death. Suffering then is necessary. It is the flame which purifies and the water which absolves. The flame burns away the dross, and one becomes cleansed by the tears of repentance for the slow ascent toward God.

Suffering, it would seem, welds one's soul in a closed circle of silence. One's unity is achieved in an inner stillness as the soul seeks to bind itself to its origin. In the "Magnificat," the great "cantique de reconnaissance," Claudel chants, "Qui participe aux volontés de Dieu, il faut qu'il participe à son silence" (III, 257). In his song of praise, he declares that he will no longer be distracted by outside interests, that his heart is turned to God. Passion has been forgotten and his spirit moves soundlessly like a river of oil in order to know God and acquire truth. The Japanese says to Rodriguez in *Soulier*: "It is written that great truths are only communicated by silence" (772). In such a state is there communication between souls, man with man, and man with God. With the shadows on the outside and a light within, the soul becomes an enclosure, a "maison fermée." Rehabilitated, the poet walks in "la terre de son après-midi" (III, 260) and desires to invade the "intelligible sojourn" of God at the post-meridian hour. Now by a silent interiorization, he attains two objectives: he is able to create—"qu'il ne reste rien de moi que la voix seule" (II, 247); and he is able to become one with God: "Soyez béni, mon Dieu, qui m'avez délivré de moi-même, / Et qui faites, que je ne place pas mon bien en moi-même . . . / Mais dans votre volonté seule, / Et non pas dans aucun bien, mais dans votre volonté seule" (III, 257).

In a commentary on *Soulier de Satin,* Claudel cites the Portuguese saying: "Deus escreve direite por linhas tortas" ["God writes straight in crooked lines"] (*Théâtre,* II, 1308). Everything, even evil, has its meaning in the ultimate purpose and plan. Man wonders why the disorder, why the conflicts, what indeed is the meaning and purpose of this absurd life? Besme in *La Ville* reveals his alienation and disenchantment by iterating "Rien n'est."[9] His doubt exceeds the beauty and joy of Coeuvre's universe. All of his knowledge fails to enlighten his spirit. He is encumbered by his fear of death. He has touched the "horreur de l'inutilité" in life, and to live for him has become a mockery. Yet, it is by faith, the chemistry of salvation, that doubt is obliterated; it is the force which enables one to endure. The image of Christ on the Cross restores one's ability to accept pain, frustration, betrayal. Humanity bears no cross greater than that to which His body was affixed; humanity has no sins to which his wounds do not correspond (*Chemin de la Croix,* 493). It is for this reason, Claudel intones, that we must bear the cross before it will bear us (*Chemin,* 484). Hence the suffering of both saints and sinners.

Death provides the "affranchissement," the ultimate deliverance; the eternal part of oneself is finally liberated. Scarcely does the poet overlook any aspect of death from the final physical suffering to the union with the community of saints. The chief motif is that death brings everything to life; it does not conquer life, it is destroyed by life (III, 253).

Claudel affirms, as did Pascal, the fragility of God's creature,

9. *Theatre,* II (Version II), 440–41. All references from *La Ville* are from this edition.

the weakest thing in nature: "Ah, comme c'est donc fragile, un être humain!" (*La Messe*, 503). When in *Tête d'Or* Simon defies death, Cébès reveals his fear of the future and the horrors of life by cataloguing the diseases to which the flesh is subject:

> Toutes les maladies veillent sur nous, l'ulcère et l'abcès, l'épilepsie et le hochement de la tête, et à la fin vient la goutte et la gravelle qui empêche de pisser.
> La phtisie fait son feu; les parties honteuses moisissent comme du raisin; et le sac de ventre,
> Crève et vide dehors les entrailles et les excréments!
> N'est-ce pas horrible? mais notre vie
> Qui se fait de fête à un repas de larve s'empiffre,
> Jusqu'à ce que, comme un chien qui vomit des vers et des morceaux de viande,
> Le ventre bourré se révolte et qu'on rende gorge sur la table! (*Théâtre*, I, 180)

When the enormity of pain becomes unbearable, one longs for that which Coeuvre desired: "le dernier sommeil / Du malade qui a fini même de souffrir . . ." (*Théâtre*, I, 437).

The symbol of the rose is used by the poet to illustrate the transiency of life. As soon as one seizes it, it sheds its leaves and dies. The rose is not eternal, only the aroma which is absorbed into the Eternal Essence. The body is not eternal, only the soul which is absorbed into the Eternal Spirit. Beata, in the "Cantique de la Rose," knows that reality blooms for one moment beneath the fragile veils: "C'est la réalité un instant pour nous qui éclot sous ces voiles fragiles . . . / Ah, qu'au milieu de l'année cet instant est fragile . . .!" (*Cantate*, 334–35). The moment of the summer solstice symbolizes the brevity of life. For herself and her sisters, Beata wishes that they might be a rose in the arms of their lovers, since the important thing for her is not to live but to die and be "consommé" in the act of love.

Intertwined in each reference to death is the theme that death brings everything to life, and that one dies to bloom again in another garden. The immortal element in man demands to die, to seek its source, to find its roots in heaven. Claudel explains this reaching for origin on the part of man as follows: "Proprement humain est donc ce que j'appellerai sentiment de la tige; le sentiment de l'origine, le sentiment religieux (*religare*), le mystérieux attachement placentaire" (*Art Poétique*, 184). Man's death gives meaning to existence since it attests that God the Maker lives (*La Messe*, 500). It is the faithful then who experience joy at the moment of death. As a drop of water is absorbed by the sea, so are the faithful absorbed in the communion of saints. The dogma of the communion of saints teaches that all souls with the same vision will know each other (*Art Poétique*, 199–200). Each spirit recognizes other necessary and complementary spirits. Each soul also knows God by the image of God repeated in itself. It becomes affixed to and rooted in the Source by the power of love. In its vibration, awareness of other homogeneous substances develops (*Art Poétique*, 200–3). The solidarity of souls thus repeats the solidarity of mankind, an expression of unity in God's creation.

In "Commémoration des fidèles trépassés" (*Corona Benignitatis Anni Dei*) Claudel meditates on God's regret because of His creation of sinful man. In the commemorative ritual for all of the faithful dead, one's own death is fearfully anticipated. The reading of the *Miserere* evokes the memory of innumerable persons whose souls are naked face to face with God. More terrible than any temporal suffering is the purgation of the soul for its entry into paradise. Anticipating the suffering in purgatory, an attempt is made to justify one's actions before the final rupture. A defiant and accusing question is uttered: "Est-ce que Tu trouves digne de Toi de me suivre ainsi? / Epiant la chose que je vais faire . . . ?" Then follows an expression of fear, an acknowledgment of guilt, a plea for a moment's respite, and finally acquiescence: "Moi qui vais être détruit dans un moment comme un vêtement qui est mangé par les cancrelats! . . . / Et c'est vrai que mes péchés sont grands . . . / Laisse-moi en repos un moment, éloigne-Toi de moi un peu/Le temps que j'avale ma salive! / . . . Entends le cri de Tes petits qu'on tue et le silence de l'enfant qui n'est pas coupable . . . / Ça ne fait rien, ô mon Dieu, et je sais bien que ça n'est pas Votre faute! . . . Et quand Vous me damneriez, je sais que Vous êtes mon Créateur! / Vous êtes mon Père tout de même!" (*Oeuvre Poétique*, 465–66). Such are the reflections of the living as they perform their duty toward the dead.

VII. Inner Reality
and Outer Vision

What is reality? Is it tangible or intangible? Is it sensed by the senses, intuited by the mind, or is there a fusion of all faculties of cognition? Answers to these questions have been proposed through the years by the philosophers. An immediate and pedestrian response is that reality is tangible. It can be seen, heard, touched, tasted, and smelled. The questions here however are, What is real for the poet? What, to him, is the essence of the universe?

The irrefutable premise of both Claudel and Perse is that the world is. Claudel's "Le monde brut entier," is echoed by Perse's "Le monde entier des choses." Their purpose was to show how, in what sense, and for what reason the world is. As artists, their concern is with that which transcends phenomena, the thing in itself or the noumenon. This is the construct employed in re-creating and defining the universe. That which is sensorial furnishes the point of departure.

In the area of ideas, the poets have expressed convergent and divergent concepts. Parallel characteristics ascribed by both poets to the cosmos are as follows: movement, continuity, harmony and splendor, man in exile, the unifying power of love, human solidarity, and the existence of good and evil. One would not expect any conflict in admitting these generalities, and there are none. Differences do occur in the way of seeing, the apperceptive focus directed on creation, and in methodology. Perse's view is macrocosmic; Claudel's is microcosmic. Perse's apperception enfolds the total physical universe. Claudel's microcosmic view is concerned with the human soul.

Motion is defined and demonstrated for Perse by the movement of the planets, the swirling of the elements, and the upheavals of the ocean. Claudel, while acknowledging the same evidence, has a more philosophical approach. As explained in *Art Poétique*, the initial stages of movement are vibration and tension which exist in the most minute particles, animate and inanimate. Inner tension leads to vibration causing the exterior movement which brings each thing into contact with every other thing, giving it form and character. In regards to the soul, then, the physical universe merely mirrors it, postulates its dimensions, and establishes its connection with the Creator. The soul in its "frémissement" seeks other souls, all of which are destined to be absorbed by the Soul of the Creator.

For both poets, movement is a thrusting, explosive, frenetic action, and it is perpetual. Such movement is not haphazard, erratic, or spasmodic. There is a rhythmic and cyclical redundancy which re-creates and re-forms that which has existed from the moment that the universe was set in motion. The only fixed or static element in the concept of movement is the pattern of continuity. The principle of violence inherent in the elemental turbulence supports Perse's theme of continuous destruction. Such destruction requires re-creation, renewal, and continuity. The world is therefore in a constant state of rebirth. Natural catastrophes are merely seasonal rhythms in the vast cycle of renewal.

Redundancy and the principle of irreversibility confer a beauty of their own on the physical world. Perse testifies to the constancy of nature when he speaks of recurring dawns whose garments never change. The fact of physical interdependence and intermeshing in the repetitive movement enhances the concept of splendor. Harmony results from the interlocking of forms, colors, and sounds. It is this one law of harmony, according to Perse, which governs the universe. Believers and nonbelievers are compelled to wonder why as they contemplate the masked and resistant universe. Unable to know really, the poet acclaims its beauty and splendor. Fundamentally, this is the position taken by Perse who glorifies the majesty of the sea, extols the power of the elements, and honors the cyclical movements of the cosmos.

What is the source of the redundant, perpetual and harmonic movements? Perse's point of view is that the source of a thing is found in the thing itself. The beginning and the end, the creator and the created are all one in the visible world. All creation is earthbound. He views the world in movement with itself as the goal. There is no "other world" in the Christian sense. Claudel sees the world in movement with a fixed and divine purpose—the revelation of the existence of God. In his dissertation on Cause in *Connaissance du Temps*, Claudel seems to refute the yet-to-be stated theory of Perse on origin: When one sees in a single thing the ensemble of causes and effects, one concludes that the same law which orders the existence of things also brought them into being, and that each thing is infused with an irrepressibly determined generative virtue (*Art Poetique*, 131). The so-called law that one deduces to explain phenomena, Claudel dismisses as simply a means of intellectual assimilation (*Art Poétique*, 132). Also, he regards as an absurdity the idea of perpetual movement which has no source and no purpose: "Qu'est-ce donc que cette force privée de source, cette machine qui se nourrit et se produit elle-même? Joujou, qui va, sans objet que son mouvement même, par la seule impuissance à s'arrêter. Voici l'automate éternel dansant indéfiniment!" (*Art Poetique*, 134).

It seems fairly evident that both poets concur on the principle and pattern of movement as a dynamic and creative necessity, although they differ as to origin and purpose. Perse sees only the physical phenomenon and ascribes to it a symbolic reflection of man and his activities. Claudel sees the physical phenomenon as a necessary part of the totality and unity of things born in the mind of God. Totality and unity are made manifest by the interdependence and the interrelationship of natural forces whose concurrence makes continuity possible. The unity and interdependence of the physical world are evident since nothing can or does exist in a static vacuum. Interaction is necessary because nothing comes into existence alone; there is a simultaneous birth, a "co-naissance" of all being. Although Perse does not recognize any divine link, he does support the above point of view. Nothing, he states, is born from nothingness, nor to nothingness is joined. This is in accord with Parmenidian theory that being does not come from non-being, and that there is no void in the universe.

The universe in perpetual movement is the undecipherable poem that God writes. The poet also becomes creator in his attempt to break the code. This is the mystery with which he is confronted when he observes the totality of creation and presumes to assign meaning to that which is transcendent. The continuous outer movement and inner vibration constitute the being and becoming of this finite universe in a constant state of re-creation.

Though myriad and multifarious in form and number, though endowed with varying quantities of energy, each element is linked to every other element by the Divine Essence which confers unity on all of creation. This idea of Claudel is further explored in "La Légende de Prakriti." Specifically, he points out a sort of lateral obligation on the part of plants and animals to furnish to each other aid, nourishment, resection, or anything indispensable for their well-being.[1] The collaboration of plants and animals affirms the solidarity of the natural world. Human solidarity is the obvious corollary. Man, as the summit, the splendor, and the crowning achievement of creation, possessing a soul and the power of expression, has the obligation to establish and maintain the solidarity of mankind. The solidarity of the

1. *Figures et Paraboles* (Paris, 1936), p. 138.

animate and of the inanimate is essential for the completion of the unity of the universe.

It is difficult to deny the unity of mankind, prevailing conditions notwithstanding. Man is bound to man by necessity. Claudel and Perse agree on the fundamentals of human solidarity as seen in the will to procreate, to survive, to improve the environment by controlling the forces of nature, and ultimately to conquer the universe. Each of these terms—survival, improving the environment, conquering the universe—has a different connotation for the two poets. The unity of mankind is preserved by a wave of spiritual energy which pervades and permeates the cosmos. Perse's "wave of spiritual energy" is Claudel's "presence of God" both of which insure the affinity of all created things.

The unity of mankind encompasses the socio-physical and the psychical. Evidence of the socio-physical unity of mankind is recognized in Perse's processions of civilizations of the East and of the West, of the past and of the present. The gregarious masses move ahead in time and space, increasing their numbers and expanding their world. In *Vents*, he details the westward movement of men of all types, trades, professions, and interests. They are drawn, as though mesmerized, by the promise of broad expanses of land, and beyond, by the promise of the broad expanses of the sea. In their mind, they foresee prodigious actions as they proceed to subdue, modify, and discipline their natural and social environment. Because of their intelligence they succeed in exploiting the treasures above and beneath the earth, harnessing the force of the rivers, establishing great cities and socio-political enclaves. The improvement of the environment results directly from technological inventions, innovations and discoveries which have accrued through the centuries. Man's mastery over matter testifies to the splendor of his intellect. All of his energy is dedicated to the development of a more efficient material world to serve the needs of the strong and those who are able to survive.

Perse portrays mankind as "les grands Itinérants du songe et de l'action" being constantly propelled by the winds of ambition. In another sense, the winds are designated as great forces of insult, discord, license, error, sophistry, anger, wrangling, intolerance, and violence which drive and infest man's spirit. These are the forces which leave their imprint on his affairs and in his heart. In *Chronique* the poet invokes the night to heed the wandering footstep of the soul without a refuge (II, 342). His era is reduced to dust and decay. Yet, infested by the dream, man persists, and the cycle of creation begins again. Refreshed by the storm, once more man becomes inhabited by "la force vive et l'idée neuve" and rebuilds on the rubble of the past.

Thus does the poet come to terms with life as he assesses its upheavals. After devastating shocks, catastrophes, and personal loss, the being is purified in the same manner that the land is cleansed by wind and rain and set afire by lightning. Vigée speaks of this analogy when he writes that Perse implies a purification of the creative poetic conscience by exile, water, and fire which in its fresh state is able to rejoin the Source.[2]

Claudel's reference to the socio-physical unity of mankind as reflected in his culture is not designed to glorify the handiwork and intellect of man as in the case of Perse. Rather, he reveals the vanity of worldly pursuits. Man is of course bound by his need to survive and unites his efforts to that end, with his attention riveted on secular goals. He synthesizes its resources for his well-being. For this, Claudel asserts, he received the benediction of the first five days preceding his own creation. Yet, it is this kind of limited concentration which leads to his enslavement by ideologies and things. In his encounter with the Muse "qui est la Grâce," Claudel proclaims his desire to establish himself as an accountant of humanity and his wish to sing of terrestrial matters. He begs to write the great poem of man as he makes his triumphant march across the face of the earth, as Perse later succeeded in doing. Disabused by the Muse, he finally renounces the task of chronicler for that of a higher duty, that of revealing God's presence in the temporal world.

Henceforth, he concerns himself with the contingent in order to understand and assimilate this world with the divine. He declares his disdain for machines and technological progress, his scorn for laurel-crowned Caesars and their effort to conquer the world for themselves. He recounts, in indignation, the deeds of

2. *Révolte et Louanges* (Paris, 1962), pp. 209-11.

the powerful who seek to crush the Christian faith. They have become obscene masks at his feet. He wishes that all of the work of mankind would be subjected to the unifying grace of God. Such an affinity would attest to His presence.

The physical unity of man is an uncontested fact; the psychical unity of mankind remains to be achieved. This is the preoccupation of the poet who has deep concern for the human condition. Perse speaks of the permanence and unity of Being with which the poet establishes a liaison for the benefit of mankind. He desires that the collective soul be more closely bound to the prevailing wave of spiritual energy so that temporal and non-temporal (spiritual) man may not be forever alienated (*Poésie*, 17–18). The waves of spiritual energy are the pervading and permeating forces of the cosmos which must be harnessed in order to establish and preserve the solidarity of man. In the Chorus of *Amers*, "Mer de Baal, Mer de Mammon," Perse addresses the sea as the wandering one of blind migration. Along her trails and pathways, she, the federal sea and sea of alliance will lead her hordes of diverse people toward a distant fusion into a single race of mankind (II, 305).

Psychical unity, an original characteristic of man, was destroyed by original sin, from the Christian point of view. From the secular viewpoint, this unity has been nullified by historical forces and social pressures. Individual man suffers from personal disunity, alienation from self and society, and a spiritual void. Evidence of man's state of exile and alienation is seen in what has been termed his "passion for depravity," his indulgence in violence, and his tolerance of it which is as debasing as violence itself. Strife seems to be a way of life for civilized man. It seems to generate more from greed than from need. There is the constant and competitive striving for things, land, nations, peoples, and the minds of people. With some reservations, one must agree with Rousseau when he says that the first person to stake out a piece of land and call it his was responsible for the establishment of civil society and its attendant evils: crime, war, genocide, and other forms of violence. The turmoil of the world reflects itself in the turmoil of the soul. Man's intelligence tells him that something is wrong. He seems powerless to act; and in a state of frustration he begins to believe that the whole business of living is absurd. Life devolves into a cipher of nothingness, and the void in man deepens.

A veneer of conformism, a patina of self-deception, and a thick stratum of indifference to the life of the spirit have been superimposed on the inner man, the fundamental self, and one's identity becomes buried. The question is asked, Who am I? In *Art Poétique*, Claudel reassures: ". . . l'homme est encore nu! sous le vêtement immonde, il est pur comme une pierre!" (p. 132). Artists have long been aware of the hidden and imprisoned "real" being, and have been scraping away at the mask. The task has been as difficult as that of deciphering the mystery and removing the mask of the physical world. Although Perse extols the intellect of man, he laments his material bondage. Poetry, he hopes, will illumine the darkness of his soul. The enlightenment that Perse would bring is the revelation to man of his spiritual possibilities so that he would be a more unified, productive, and fulfilled creature in this world. Enlightenment on the part of Claudel is of course the light of the eternal presence of God in the heart of man. When individual man becomes unified, the integrity, the oneness, the wholeness of mankind will be assured.

Both Claudel and Perse propose a means for the realization of personal and collective unity. The answer is love, cosmic and divine, which is symbolized in great detail in their sensuous evocations of physical or conjugal love. Many aspects of sexuality are explored to reveal its role in the evolution of the individual to a spiritual state. The two poets ascribe a divine characteristic to woman. Perse says that woman is marked by the divine standard and bears the stamp of the gods. Claudel goes further than this when he states that woman is the symbol of spiritual entities and represents the Church, divine grace, and sacred wisdom. As such, she is the link between man and God. She is the natural complement of man who is bound to her and bears on his stomach the seal of his attachment.

The configuration of love between man and woman, in Claudel's view, involves passionate consummation, re-creation, and more often, sacrifice of personal desire for the salvation of one's soul. Sacrifice and renunciation for another's salvation or for an ultimate good mirror divine love whose restorative effect is one of conciliation: that of man with himself, with his world, and with his Creator. Love from Claudel's God filters down and fills the heart of every receptive believer, who in turn must pass it on for the fulfillment of divine purpose.

In Perse's world, love involves neither personal sacrifice nor renunciation. It is the ultimate and mutual fulfillment; it is an approach to the Source;: it is the force which generates power and life as do the waves of the sea. The sea is the real and symbolized matrix of Being in which everything is unified. Immersion in the water purifies man, and he sees the reflection of his divinity. The poet seeks to make man aware of his original self. He wants him to recapture his spirituality through love in order to realize his destiny on earth. It is woman who perceives an estrangement in the eyes of man and becomes anxious about his wandering heart. In "Etroits sont les vaisseaux," she broods: "La nuit où tu navigues n'aura-t-elle point son île, son rivage? Qui donc en toi toujours s'aliène et se renie?" (II, 232).

Once man, individually and collectively, becomes suffused with love and aware of his spirituality, ecumenism will become more than a popular theological term. Disorder and ugliness, within and without, will be eradicated, and the solidarity of man through cosmic and psychical unity will be established. This is the poet's dream as he meditates on the confused conditions of the world.

As interpreters of the universe, Perse and Claudel project the future as mankind moves toward the achievement of spiritual unity. The new world of Perse will be inhabited by new men reintegrated and rehabilitated after the decay has been sluiced away. As men of action, their pride will be in the striving, not in the using or the having; their purpose will be to grow, not to build. The poet cites the need for men of wisdom and men of talent who must contribute or be destroyed; there must be men with new ideas and men skilled in dealing with men. The wave of spiritual energy of which he continually speaks is the dominating influence of his new world. Human energy invested with spirituality is to be expended for human progress and maintain in man's mind the value and significance of the human presence in the universe.

Teilhard de Chardin discusses convincingly the evolution and destiny of man. There is an alliance between his ideas and Perse's thought in spite of Chardin's Catholic orientation, just as there is with Claudel's. Chardin's theory is that humanity is not an accidental phenomenon, but a characteristic form of the cosmic phenomenon.[3] The continuity of the cosmos assures the continuity and thus the future of man. Chardin speaks of the efficacy of human energy in disciplining the determinism of matter, thus leading to progress in the conquest of the universe. The activity of man is also evident in the continuing effort to extend the bonds of his social unity. In addition to physical and social achievements, man's personality will be exalted. The three columns set forth by Chardin as the direction of human destiny are: futurism, universalism, and personalism.[4]

In different language, the above ideas seem to constitute Perse's belief about the future, the solidarity of mankind, and the spiritualization of man's personality. It appears that he stops short of the third stage of Chardin's curve in the evolution of man: Pre-Life, Life, Thought. He does not set Thought, the final evolutionary stage, apart as a separate entity. It is thought which will create and maintain the spirituality of life and lead to human perfectibility. Thought, as the manifestation of the life of the spirit, will establish the pattern of grandeur envisioned by the poet. He asks: ". . . connaît-on bien l'espèce où nous nous avançons?" (*Chronique*, II, 328). Self-determination, then, lies within man's choices. His future lies within himself and within the present. The Patrician women of *Amers* speak of the memory of a palace and a country of the future (II, 187). The poet further asserts that those who shall die will proclaim one day that man is immortal in the "foyer" of the moment (II, 318). In *Chronique*, he says that in vain does death cross man's path; his road lies beyond: "O Mort . . . tu croises en vain nos sentes bos-

3. "Sauvons l'humanité," *Cahiers Pierre Teilhard de Chardin* (Paris, 1962), III, 73.
4. Ibid., pp. 74–79.

selées d'os, car notre route tend plus loin . . . nous vivons d'outre-mort, et de mort même vivrons-nous" (II, 324).

Claudel proposes similar ideas about self-determination and the future. Man is "soustrait au hasard" and can determine his mode of action, his future destiny. The Jesuit Father of *Soulier* in an opening prayer acknowledges that the past and future are the same and together form "une seule étoffe indéchirable." It is the present which is man's eternity within the enclosed boundary of Time whose very center is eternal.[5] Within this closed circle, he determines his future by his present interests and concern. The idea of human progress through human effort is not at all incompatible with Christian tenets. Any human act which simulates divine creativity is, in Claudel's view, meritorious. Christ exhorts man to use his God-given talents as a testimony to his divinely inherent traits. Everything in nature is designed for and addressed to man, the coordinating point in the physical world. His intelligence, therefore, must be applied to an analysis of his environment. In the same manner that the poet orders the universe by his art, man disciplines nature for human uses by his intellect.

Both poets agree then that man is the new Prometheus, Perse with praise, and Claudel with regret. Claudel's regret is because of the secular limitations of man's activity. When Besme, in his dialogue with Coeuvre in *La Ville*, boasts of the accomplishments of man, Coeuvre satirically concurs that he is the "profond mime/ Pénétrant en les imitant les mouvements les plus secrets de la nature, / Tu les fis servir aux usages humains" (p. 429). He goes on to predict that one day man will put the planets to work as though they were mules, that the force of the oceans would run the turbines, and that the repercussion of light would grind grain and weave fabrics. Besme agrees with him and catalogs his activities as Father of the city. He confesses, however, that even as he assesses his mastery over matter, he is overwhelmed from time to time by the bitter thought of the finality of death. And as he walks through the city at night contemplating his handiwork, he considers it a derisive and funereal habitation, and believes that man will never escape from the

5. *Traité de la Co-Naissance, Oeuvre Poétique* (Paris, 1957), p. 203.

sepulchre which he has constructed for himself (*La Ville*, 429–32).

It would seem that Claudel and Perse espouse eighteenth-century anthropocentrism, with its implication of the perfectibility of human existence. The perfectibility of man establishes the limitations of his evolution for Perse; while from Claudel's standpoint, the perfectibility of temporal man is but a step toward the perfectibility of the soul. As a matter of fact, in *Connaissance du Temps*, he says that he does not envisage the future; his design is to decipher the present. The future of man in his universe is the survival of the soul after the demise of the body. Mankind must contribute to the re-creative act by adding something of himself, thereby growing spiritually by that which he gives. This is the way of assuring continuity on the human level and also that of entering on the pathway to Grace.

VIII. The Language
of Inner Vision

꽃

The greatest similarity between Claudel and Perse
lies perhaps in their use of language. Wallace Fowlie in *Climate
of Violence* indicates this: "The poetry of Saint-John Perse has
affiliations with certain formal rhetorical aspects of Claudel's
work. . . ."[1] A similar affinity is pointed out by Alain Bosquet in
his discussion of the relationship between the two poets: "One
could say that the verset of Saint-John Perse presented more
than an analogy with that of Paul Claudel, and that the tone of
Anabase sometimes approached that of the *Grandes Odes*."[2]
Roger Caillois recognizes no filiation between the work of Perse
and that of any other poet.[3] Tone and image as created by lan-

1. (New York, 1967), p. 88.
2. *Saint-John Perse* (Paris, 1953), p. 95.
3. *Poétique de Saint-John Perse* (Paris, 1954), p. 13. Caillois presents
a detailed lexical and syntactical analysis of the poet's work. He discusses
Perse's use of language in creating certain images and rhythms. There is
no discussion of the author, his inspiration, or his purpose. Gérald Antoine

guage are the broad areas chosen for comparison since they are the aspects which make up the character of the poetic work.

The hallmark of the true literary artist, the establishment of an alliance between thought and language, idea and form, is almost total in the work of Claudel and Perse. Their choice and manipulation of language reveal their virtuosity in achieving a significant rapport. This rapport is evident, in the first instance, by the manner in which the language of the poetic work recreates the universe. In fact, the poem becomes the universe. Quite literally, one finds some of everything, and this could scarcely be otherwise in view of the poets' preoccupation with the entire world of things with man at the center and the reason for it all. Their verbal repertory is sometimes baroque, sensuous, commonplace, and most often erudite and hermetic.

A great deal of the criticism toward the works of Perse and Claudel stems from what is considered their unintelligibility. In *Poésie*, Perse ascribes the obscurity for which poets are reproached to the darkness of that which they seek to explore. The darkness is the night of the soul itself and the mystery in which man is immersed (p. 16). Pierre Moreau recounts that, as early as 1892, Claudel's father had requested his son's new friend, Maurice Pottecher, to assist the poet with his style: ". . . to correct his errors, his distressing obscurities, complications, extravagances of his style and of his conceptions."[4] Claudel had recently published *Tête d'Or*. In "La Maison Fermée," Claudel acknowledges the reproach addressed to him because of an apparent alienation from man's need due to his language and style: "Est-ce langage d'un homme ou de quelque bête? . . . / Mais tu retournes et brouilles tout dans le ressac de tes vers entremêlés . . ." (V, 278).

In order to justify his use of a personal technique for more than forty years, Claudel wrote "Sur le vers français" in which he presents some fundamentals of his poetics. This work is more accessible to the casual reader than his *Art Poétique*. A full ap-

---

has made a similar but less technical study of the poetic devices of Claudel in *Les Cinq Grandes Odes ou la poésie de la répétition* (Paris, 1959). There are allusions to the inspiration and purpose of the author.

4. "A Propos de la 'Correspondance Claudel-Pottecher,'" *Cahiers Paul Claudel* (Paris, 1959), I, 61.

preciation of Claudel necessitates an attunement to his religious philosophy. More than this, one must understand his theory about words, their psychology, their function in the space on the page, and their physiological utterance. In the essay, he points out that ideas are anterior to words and therefore create or choose the words. These words must be agreeable to the spirit and to the physiological organs of expression if they are to make real the function of poetry—joy. The rhythmic beat of the heart furnishes the basic iambic meter, "un temps faible et un temps fort." Added to this rhythm is the rhythmic process of inhalation and exhalation. The poet makes use of these natural rhythms furnished by an internal metronome to create free verse.[5]

Perse expresses similar points of view on the anterior function of ideas, the purpose of poetry, and natural rhythms. In *Pluies*, he says that the idea determines the tone and establishes the meter. In complimenting Valéry Larbaud for the high esteem in which he held "le plaisir" in literary art, Perse agrees that it is the very essence of the poetic principle.[6] While Claudel speaks of a natural internal metronome which gives speech its cadence, Perse, in a more abstract manner, describes the grace of poetic language which transmits the very rhythm of Being (*Poésie*, p. 15).

Free verse, resembling the language of the Psalms and of the Biblical prophets, is the metric form possessing the suppleness and vivacity so much admired by Claudel. The possibilities and advantages of "vers libre" are implied in the questions of the apprentice-poet in Claudel's essay:

Comment faire . . . pour garder cette franchise, cette liberté, cette vivacité, cet éclat du langage parlé, et cependant pour lui donner cette consistance et cette organisation intérieure qu'exige l'inscription sur le papier? Comment ouvrir à la Muse un chemin de roses? comment l'enivrer sans la rassasier jamais d'une musique qui ait à la fois l'intérêt de la recherche et la douceur de l'autorité? comment garder le rêve en écartant le sommeil? comment soutenir son pas d'un nombre à la fois sensible et introuvable comme le coeur?[7]

5. *Positions et Propositions* (Paris, 1928), I, 11–13.
6. "Message pour Valéry Larbaud," *Les Cahiers de la Pléiade*, 13 (Autumn 1951–Spring 1952), 12.
7. *Positions et Propositions*, I, 60.

Claudel gives an explanation to the apprentice-poet who also marvels at the musicality of the unaffected language of two women who are hidden from view. Such natural speech, he says, is a latent form of poetry in its raw form. It has the sonority, the spontaneity, the pauses and the cadences of free verse. The "Tragédiennes" of Perse in *Amers* also seek an alliance with the language of the people. Perse asserts that poetry is an irreducible part of man; it existed in the cave man and exists in the man of the atomic age (*Poésie*, p. 15). It may be added that poetry exists in the language of the lunar age as demonstrated by Neil Armstrong who said as he stepped on the surface of the moon: "That's one small step for [a] man, one giant leap for mankind" (July 20, 1969).

Although Claudel found much to admire in classical poetry, he rejected the alexandrine line because of its artificiality and the restraints imposed upon natural utterance. Many seventeenth-century poets, preoccupied with primary rhythms and homophonic sonorities failed to utilize the internal sonorities and the natural and delightful resources of the French language. The rigidity of the verse form restricted fantasy, passion, music, and became a cerebral exercise.[8] A prosodic convention in the last dramas of Shakespeare, "l'enjambement," was admired and practiced by Claudel. The breaking of syllables, words, and lines produces force and vivacity in free verse thus giving it the quality of natural speech. This practice permits words to acquire a tension and forces a sense of expectation to rise in the reader. The reader's apperception of the syllables, words, and lines involves him in an active participation in the creation of the image.

The disposition of the irregular lines of free verse and the isolated words or syllables surrounded by blank space strengthen observation and comprehension. This blank space represents the unspoken thought. Further, it creates a graphic image of the emotion which precedes, accompanies, and follows the words. A line followed by a blank space involves a double action: ". . . cette respiration par laquelle l'homme absorbe la vie et restitue une parole intelligible."[9] Claudel elaborates his idea on the sig-

8. Ibid., p. 22.
9. Ibid., p. 64.

nificance of blank space on the page in another essay, "Philoso-phie du Livre." There is, he states, a musical rapport between the spoken word and silence. The silence afforded by the exis-tence of the blank space is a condition of the existence of the poetic line which stops at a certain point because the interior rhythm, "le chiffre intérieur," has been completed. This idea is based to some extent on Mallarmeian theory of "le plein et le vide" and the significance given the affirmation by the surround-ing space.[10] In "Les Muses," he repeats that the poem is not made of letters, but of the space which remains on the paper.

When one reads Perse, it seems that the poet endorses the poetics of Claudel. If any work other than the Nobel prize acceptance speech, *Poésie*, can be said to express the poetic theory of Perse, it is *Oiseaux*.[11] The insistent and long solicitation that he ascribes to Braque in his depiction of a bird's flight is that of Perse himself,[12] and is perhaps the best definition of his poetry. Braque's birds in space are Perse's words on the page or an image in the limitless territory of creative thought. Perse equates the word with the free flight of the bird which is a poetry of action and more supple than time. In the incandescent purity of its flight, there is grace and passion. It breaks the thread of gravitation to soar, and in a single thrust reaches the limits of flight as it joins the luminous energy of outer space (pp. 21–22). With all things errant throughout the world, the birds go where goes the very movement of things, where goes the very course of the sky on its wheel, to an immensity of living and creating (p. 33). They cling to the invisible strata of the sky, princes of ubiquity, searching affinity in a very certain and vertiginous "non-lieu," mimicking there a wing-tip of flame or two leaves in the wind (pp. 29–30).

On the page of the sky, the bird enjoys the privilege of being both the bow and the arrow of flight, the theme and the purpose (p. 17). Perse devotes all of part eight of *Oiseaux* to a direct

---

10. Ibid., pp. 120–22.
11. (Paris, 1963). All references to *Oiseaux* in the text are from this edition.
12. Alain Jouffroy, "Entre demi-dieux," *L'Express*, February 13, 1964, p. 25.

analogy between birds and words to illustrate their power. Words, moving toward maturity, develop in a poetic work with vigor and originality. With their magic charge, they are the nuclei of force and action, bearing afar the initiative and the premonition. On the white page with its infinite margins, the space that they measure is only an incantation. In the meter they are syllabic quantities. Proceeding from a far-distant origin, they lose their meaning at the limits of happiness. Vocables, subjected to the same concatenation, they exercise a new divination in foretelling the future. Words, resembling the wooden bird used by ancient scribes for medium-like writing, are borne by a universal rhythm and inscribe themselves in the broadest strophe that has ever been unfolded (pp. 23–24).

The manner in which the poet utilizes the resources and potential of lexical units determines the effectiveness of free verse. Implications from the poetics of both Claudel and Perse show that the word is a free and volatile element, an important component for artistic creativity. The freedom of the poet makes possible the free play given to words. Claudel makes many references to the freedom possessed by the truly creative artist. The liberty of the poet is identified by him with the liberty of God; and along with Perse, he also identifies this liberty with that of the omnipresent sea. Both poets had experienced the "rapt" and the "spasme mortel" which brought about their poetic expression. In "La Muse qui est la Grâce," Claudel writes of working in a trance and of the movement of the spirit which with a "spasme mortel" thrusts the word out of him as a source aware only of its pressure and the weight of the sky (IV, 275). The word thrust forth is a condensation or concentration of energy, bursting its bonds. Perse's "rapt" is symbolized by that of the painter Braque. At the moment of his "rapt" when everything is known, he sums up in a stroke the true totality of a spot of color. For painter and poet, the stroke, the word is neither sign nor symbol but the thing itself in fact and destiny, a live thing captured from the womb (*Oiseaux*, p. 13). The same idea is found in *Vents*: "Non point l'écrit, mais la chose même. Prise en son vif et dans son tout. / Conservation non des copies, mais des originaux" (II, 86). In *Amers*, Perse repeats: "Et mots pour nous ils ne sont plus, n'étant plus signes ni parures, / Mais la chose même qu'ils figurent et la chose même qu'ils paraient . . ." (II, 307–8).

The poet's conception then of the word is that it is a liberated thing, with no confining boundaries in time, space, or meaning. It is more than what it usually connotes in current usage. Particularly with Perse, the word loses nothing of its original meaning or connotation. The poet maintains the continuity. As the birds of Braque, words of ancient lineage, projected from that which is real to the limits of the unreal, fill the poetic space of man (*Oiseaux*, p. 33). It was Rivière, an early critic of the *Odes* who assessed Claudel's use of the French language. In a letter addressed to the poet in Prague in December, 1910, he wrote that Claudel's literary predecessors were the prophets and the Greeks, and that the poet revealed his ancestry only by the manner in which he handled the French language:

But the only thing by which you reveal yourself as a Frenchman, is this formidable propriety with words; it is indeed our language which you speak, and with a great precision which we did not suspect,—ordering words to produce at each instant (in order to justify their meaning) their entire past, their entire history. But justly, this very kind of violent propriety is that of someone who masters a language with genius, not that of someone who yields to it and follows it.[13]

This appraisal by Rivière indicates the confluence in the treatment of words by Claudel and Perse. Their quest for the Source parallels their recognition of original meanings of words. It is this aspect which contributes largely to the recondite nature of their poetic work.

The verbal repertory and devices employed to construct their poetic universe possess the very characteristics of the re-created cosmos. An analysis of several prosodic elements and lexical procedures followed by the poets reveals specifically the bond between language and theme.

Movement is the primary characteristic of the physical world described by the poets, and their works have the same mobile

13. Jacques Rivière and Paul Claudel, *Correspondance, 1907–1914* (Paris, 1926), p. 222.

qualities: vibrant, vigorous, explosive, effervescent, and fluid. Claudel asserts that movement is essential for poetic discourse and should be sustained by sonorous and transporting elements similar to the endless crescendos of Beethoven's first manner. There is no question but that for Perse poetry is movement, action, and power in its birth, growth, and maturity. Similar to the birds of Braque, there is nothing inert or passive; instead, poetry becomes a part of the luminous energy of the universe. Free verse as employed by both poets is a perfect form to convey their concept of poetry as movement. The meter is strengthened by the force of words such as these in the first canto of *Vents* and throughout Perse's work: "forces," "frappées," "couraient," "s'en aller," "soudain," "irruption," "éclat," "explosion," "migration," "ivresse," "assaillis," "assiégeait," "refluait," "s'engouffraient," "descellés," and "violence." A few words from Claudel's first ode, which also occur throughout his poetry, serve to support the idea of mobility: "jaillissante," "frapper," "sauter," "soudain," "déclenchait," "flambant," "enivrée," "rompre," "convulsivement," "frémissant," "déflagration," and "conflagration." In this Ode, "Les Muses," the poet addresses himself to the vibrant virgin Terpsichore whose tense, bare arm poised for movement signifies that she is ready to strike the first measure. She is the secret vowel which brings the word to life and gives movement to the poem.

Movement in the universe is evident in the proliferating abundance of the creative act. Multifarious, opulent, and fecund is the universe of Claudel and Perse; profuse, rich and generative is the language they use to describe it. There is an overflow of words, images, and symbols whose creative power reflects that of the universe. In the "Invocation" of *Amers*, which is a kind of prospectus of the work, Perse, in his description of the sea, describes the language of the poem: ". . . une langue . . . dont la phrase est nouvelle . . . grandes intumescences du langage, par grands reliefs d'images et versants d'ombres lumineuses, courant à ses splendeurs massives d'un très beau style périodique . . ." (II, 141). The poem literally presents a congestion—swollen masses of words which set forth images in bold relief. Processions in the "Invocation" form the "récitation en marche vers

l'auteur." They crowd upon each other and swell the stanza
to testify to their existence. They make up a thick slice of
history and mythology from Princes and Prophets to divine
Bastards and daughters of Stallions. Also included are the
"Messagers," "Magiciennes," and "Marchands," "Nourrices"
and "Nomades," "Prébendiers" and "Pirates," "Veuves" and
"Vierges." In "Mer de Baal, Mer de Mammon . . ." of *Amers*,
the poet acknowledges the density of his poem: "Innombrable
l'image, et le mètre, prodigue. . . . / Et maille à maille se répète
l'immense trame prosodique" (II, 296–97). Similar allusions to
density occur when he describes the sea which is the poem as:
"Mer innombrable dans ses nombres et ses multiples de nombres"
(II, 305) and "Mer utérine de nos songes et Mer hantée du
songe vrai" (II, 310). The image elicited by "Mer utérine" is
one of limitless fecundity.

   Claudel compares the overflow of his words waiting to burst
forth to that of a wet-nurse encumbered by an overflow of
milk, and to the engorgement of a river's current. Here is the
impatience of the poem experienced by both writers. When
the Muse beckons Claudel, he has need of a "hécatombe" of
words to bring into being the whole world of things. Everything
must be saluted by its name, with the word which created it.
To understand is to re-create the thing itself (III, 261). The
contingency of the universe is felt and must be expressed.

   There is a certain ordering of this overflow of words in the
creation of the poetic work. An important device for this pur-
pose is juxtaposition. In his conversation with Jean Amrouche
(*Mémoires Improvisés*), Claudel explains that the art of the
poet is in the arrangement of words in such a manner that the
desired effect will be more powerful if sustained by a concert
of other words, thus forming a new word (p. 203). Free verse,
in its similarity to speech, permits the juxtaposition of ideas and
images which leads to the creation of a new idea or image. The
facilities of Latin allowed Virgil and Pindar to juxtapose words
which had no logical rapport.[14] Claudel makes use of the device
with conglomerates of words and themes devoid of any apparent
sequence. Claudel's use of metaphor involves juxtaposing dis-

14. *Positions et Propositions*, I, 65.

parate images to create a new image or concept. The exigencies of the creative "parole" are not those of logic.

Juxtaposition as a device is particularly prominent in the many long enumerations of Perse. Caillois has a theory which purports to explain the filiation from one element to the other. He establishes lines of equivalence for both the animate and the inanimate. Elements, commonly regarded as dissimilar, may have the same atmospheric pressure, nebulosity, mean temperature, or magnetic force. Enumerations, while appearing to be haphazard, are closely connected by some common, general, or specific feature. Perse restores the bonds of a distant, common origin by presenting man engaged in particular and peculiar occupations according to his tastes and desires.[15] The man who burns bark on his roof for his pleasure, for example, may have a remote psychic kinship to the man who detects the odor of genius in the fresh crevice of the stone. The unexpected combinations and comparisons of words, phrases, images, and themes testify to the diversity and the relatedness of everything.

Although juxtaposition is the major device in their work, both poets use other devices to create and strengthen the technique itself. Among these are repetition, analogy, alliteration, figures of speech, homophonic and metagrammatic manipulations, and other syntactical variations. Juxtaposition is sometimes the result of a conscious effort for alliteration. The intermingling of several devices broadens the dimensions and augments the force of the image. Each procedure functions in relationship to the others and gives unity to the poetic symbolism of the universe. The symbolism of the universe is the poem, itself a universe. The diverseness and apparent disorder of the universe constitute fundamentally an ordered and harmonious whole when viewed through the eye of the spirit. Similarly, the genius of the poet organizes the diverseness of language and images to create a totality. The bringing together of ideas and images which are apparently unrelated offers a bewildering mélange. The poem, however, testifies to the interrelatedness of everything in the fusion of the concrete and the abstract, the real and the imaginary, the immanent and the transcendent.

15. Caillois, *Poétique de Saint-John Perse*, pp. 95, 96.

The redundant and cyclical aspects of the physical world and its continuous repetition and re-creation are mirrored by the poet in the repetition of sounds, syllables, words, phrases, and themes. Almost any work of Claudel and Perse reveals this practice. The use of repetition may have several implications. Is the poet trying to convince himself? In his musing and interiorization, does one detect doubt and uncertainty in the constant reiteration? Is what he has to express so intangible or so overwhelming that utterance is almost impossible? Repetition, however, seems to serve a less personal and more artistic purpose. The recurrence of certain forms from canto to canto emphasizes and magnifies the theme or image being presented and establishes thematic unity. On the subject of poetic inspiration in a letter to Abbé Brémond, Claudel wrote that the repetition of sounds preserves the real nature of things "la chose pure," which in the fullness of its meaning is a partial and intelligible image of God.[16] In his speech in praise of Dante, Claudel asserts that there is a *poësis perennis* which does not invent its themes, rather, it resumes eternally those furnished by Creation. Rejecting the idea of continuous evolution, he says that the true poet is content with God's handiwork and understands why nature continues to repeat each year the same rose.[17] As previously stated, Perse reiterates: "And the dawns have not yet changed their garments."

Use of the alliterative line is common to both poets for the expression of great emotion, movement, important themes, or interior accord. At times, alliteration seems to be an intentional effort to veil meanings, and again it seems to be the only means of expressing the ineffable. Claudel says that for a poet when one speaks of alliteration, of the value of consonants placed one after another, the important concern is that the consonant is the element of energy in the line. The vowel is the musical element. These three devices, juxtaposition, repetition, and alliteration reflecting as they do diversity, redundance, and accord

16. "Lettre à l'Abbé Brémond sur l'inspiration poétique," *Positions et Propositions*, I, 99–100.

17. "Introduction à un poème sur Dante," *Positions et Propositions*, I, 165–66, 169.

in the universe, dominate the poetry of Perse and Claudel. (In the following pages, a sampling from *Amers, Vents* and *Cinq Grandes Odes* is given to show similarities of style and technique. It will be immediately obvious that no attempt is made to explicate in detail.)

In *Amers,* the powerful and re-creative sea, invoked as a complete universe, rolls and swells, wallows and glides as do the hosts of history: "La Mer mouvante et qui chemine au glissement de ses grands muscles errants, la Mer gluante au glissement de plèvre . . . s'en vint à nous sur ses anneaux de python noir. . . ." This single example shows how carefully Perse chooses "le mot juste" as to sound, import, and form. There is no haphazard or arbitrary choice of the lexical item. The consonants, as Claudel suggests, are the energy-bearing elements in this alliterative line. They furnish the sense of the power and motion of the sea, tempered in its movement by its density. The sibilants in "chemine" and "glissement" present the idea of a sliding motion which is sustained by the image of the black python. The repetition of "la mer mouvante" and "la mer gluante" with the change in adjective emphasizes both density and mobility. An interior harmony is supplied by the interior rhyming of "mouvante" and "gluante" and "glissement" and "errants," the feminine rhyme embracing the masculine.

In the opening line of the poem, the poet as supplicant yearns to leave the harsh and stony realities of the land, and wonders if man will be left "parmi la pierre publique et les pampres de bronze." Here is a simple yet charged image of the character of man's civilization—his buildings and laws, his pomposity and inflexibility. The alliteration of "pierre publique" and "pampres de bronze" creates a sense of hardness, brazen artificiality, and hypocrisy. Anticipating his flight from such sterility, the poet sets the stage for an adventure of joy and a festive summer of love: "La Mer en fête sur ses marches," "la Mer en fête de nos songes," and "la Mer en fête des confins." The coming celebration is accentuated by the repetition of "fête" in the octosyllabic lines and also by its use as verb and noun in "comme fête que l'on fête."

The use in the same line of the substantive and verbal form

of the same word, very frequent in the poems of Perse, illustrates further both repetition and alliteration. The combination of past, present, and future of the same verb in the same line destroys any temporal limitations to the duration of the poem. The importance of the song is thus illustrated: "Et c'est un chant de mer comme il n'en fut jamais chanté, et c'est la Mer en nous qui le chantera." The rareness of the dream is expressed in the same structural repetition with the substitution of verb and preposition: "Et c'est un songe en mer comme il n'en fut jamais songé, et c'est la Mer en nous qui le songera." The sea within the poet will sing a song of the sea, and the sea within the poet will dream a dream within the sea. The object of the dream is inhabited by the dream—"un songe en mer," and will in turn create the reverie—"c'est la mer en nous qui le songera." It is almost impossible to capture in one's mind the elusive dream-like quality evoked by the syllables "songe en mer." "Songe de mer" would have destroyed both mood and meaning. The replacement of "chant," "chanté," and "chantera" by "songe," songé," and "songera" establishes the intermingling of utterance, dream, and source of the dream.

Other examples in the "Invocation" involving repetition by the use of noun and verb are these: "moi m'inclinant . . . d'une inclinaison," "La fumée . . . enfumera," "Et de salutation . . . serez-vous saluée," "veillent sa veille d'Etrangère," "Rêve, ô rêve tout haut ton rêve d'homme immortel!" "eut-il jamais rêvé pareille rêverie," and "comme l'oiseau vêtu de son vêtement d'ailes." Although these examples are disconnected, they convey the mood of the poet in his salutation to the sea.

Immersed in the dream of the joy to come, the poet describes the quality of the festive song in these anaphoric lines: "Poésie pour assister le chant d'une marche," "Poésie pour apaiser la fièvre d'une veille . . . / Poésie pour mieux vivre notre veille." The same type of repetition adds to the sweep of the movement: "C'est une histoire que je dirai, c'est une histoire qu'on entendra; / C'est une histoire que je dirai comme il convient qu'elle soit dite . . ."; "La Mer, en nous portée, jusqu'à la satiété du souffle et la péroraison du souffle, / La Mer, en nous, portant son bruit soyeux du large . . . / La Mer, en nous tissée, jusqu'à ses ronceraies d'abîme, la Mer, en nous tissant ses grandes heures de lumière." This kind of construction is also used to show that the freedom and limitless expanse of the sea are those of the poem: ". . . la Mer sans stèles ni portiques, sans Alyscamps ni Propylées; la Mer sans dignitaires de pierre à ses terrasses circulaires, ni rang de bêtes bâtées d'ailes à l'aplomb des chaussées." The negative aspects of freedom and life plus connotations of sadness in the funereal stelae, the roadway of tombs, the vestibules of temples, the stone statuary of dead dignitaries and winged beasts are expressed in a triple negation of harsh, alliterative sounds and syllables. Such a strong negation becomes an affirmation of joy to come.

The emotion of the poet is marked by the sensuous explosion of the exclamation "Aâh," the cry of a man at the limit of being. A deep exhalation of the breath seems to be as important to Perse as to Claudel. In *Amers*, he says that "la douceur . . . est dans l'épuisement du souffle" (II, 203). It is also seen in certain "coupes" or interruptions of the line: "Nous avons eu, nous avons eu . . . Ah! dites-le encore, était-ce bien ainsi? . . . Nous avons eu—et ce fut telle splendeur de fiels et de vins noirs!" This is a rather strange and unsavory image, in the manner of Baudelaire—the splendor of gall and black wine. Both nouns are repulsive, and Perse amplifies their intensity by the use of "splendeur." This line follows the depiction of a place of sacred offerings covered with blood and the visceral remains of sacrificial animals. The wandering sea is observed as it is caught in the trap of its aberration.

The invocation addressed to the sea for guidance and inspiration has many phrases of solicitation: "Inonde, ô brise, ma naissance!," "Guide-moi, plaisir, sur les chemins de toute mer," "Commande, ô fifre, l'action, et cette grâce encore d'un amour qui ne nous mette en mains que les glaives de joie!" Numerous are the comparisons to be found in the description of the sea and thereby of the poem. The sea is like a divine promulgation; it is as immense and as green as the dawn; it is all license, all birth, all resipiscence, a tree of light, a luminous page against the night.

These examples taken from the "Invocation" of *Amers* repre-

sent a few of the poetic devices in the total poem. A complete
and detailed explication would reveal almost every possible
prosodic technique. The same techniques are found in *Vents*.
Examples from Canto I will partially index devices used in the
remaining cantos of the poem.

Repetition in *Vents* parallels the incessant blowing of the
winds: "C'étaient de très grands vents sur toutes faces de ce
monde, / De très grands vents en liesse par le monde . . . / . . .
de très grands vents sur toutes faces de vivants! . . . / C'étaient
de très grands vents en quête sur toutes pistes de ce monde . . . /
Sur toutes choses périssables, sur toutes choses saisissables, parmi
le monde entier des choses . . . ," "Flairant la pourpre, le cilice,
flairant l'ivoire et le tesson, flairant le monde entier des choses."
These several examples occur in the first few lines, underscoring
the insistence of the poet on the persistence and the scope of
the winds. The last line offers two examples of antithesis. In "la
pourpre" and "le cilice" there is the pride of royal robes and the
humility of the hair-shirt. One is aware of the durability of
"l'ivoire" and the fragility of "le tesson." The phrase "le monde
entier des choses" occurs throughout the poem indicating the
dimensions of the poet's quest.

In the same canto, a decadent century is compared to a tree
in the following repetitive and alliterative phrases with varia-
tions: "Car tout un siècle s'ébruitait dans la sécheresse de sa
paille, parmi d'étranges désinences: à bout de cosses, de siliques
. . . / Comme un grand arbre sous ses hardes et ses haillons de
l'autre hiver, portant livrée de l'année morte; / Comme un grand
arbre tressaillant dans ses crécelles de bois mort et ses corolles
de terre cuite—. . . / Comme ce grand arbre de magie sous sa
pouillerie d'hiver . . . / Ha! très grand arbre du langage peuplé
d'oracles." Several of the preceding quotes are examples of
anaphora with the repetition of the same word to begin each
line or phrase. The two stanzas in which reference is made to the
tree fairly crackle with that which is dead or decayed and des-
tined to be blown away: "sécheresse de paille," "cosses," "sili-
ques," "haillons," "crécelles de bois morte," "corolles de terre
cuite," "dépouilles et spectres de locustes," "filiales d'ailes." The
page itself rustles as something dead and brittle. In the enumera-

tion there is the juxtaposition of plants, insects, earth, time, and language. Startling effects are produced in some analogies and comparisons: "Parole brève comme éclat d'os." The brevity, sharpness, and nakedness of a word are compared to the splintering of bone. These phrases, "comme un grand pan de croyance morte, comme un grand pan de robe vaine et de membrane fausse—" which speak of dead faith, an empty robe, and false membranes create an image of death and decadence.

A line that is repeated and which testifies to the impatience of the song to be born is "Se hâter, se hâter! Parole de vivant!" The depths to which the poet must go is emphasized by the repeated invocation, "Eâ, dieu de l'abîme." Men are "assaillis du dieu" and have their face in the wind as does the poet. An effort is made to seduce the Muse with the repeated "O toi, désir, qui vas chanter" and "Et toi, désir, qui vas chanter." The favor of the god is sought for the song and the vision: "Faveur du dieu sur mon poème!," "Favorisé du songe favorable," "O vous que rafraîchit l'orage . . . Fraîcheur et gage de fraîcheur." Repetition with slight lexical changes or combination of noun and adjective, synonyms, verb and noun derivatives, or metagrammatic changes elaborates the sense of the image. Here are some examples: "silence et silencieux offices," "spores et sporules de lichens," "songeait les songes," "Nous y levons face nouvelle, nous y lavons face nouvelle," "sous l'étirement du rire," "sous l'étirement du soir." In the appraisal of a library, the poet writes: "Et les murs sont d'agate où se lustrent les lampes" and "Et les murs sont d'agate où s'illustrent les lampes." Two related verb forms are used and the sibilance is maintained.

Alliteration which reinforces and sometimes presents the quality of a dream or reality is seen in these expressions: "feu des forges," "lit de luxure," "filiales d'ailes et d'essaim," "fille d'ailes se fit l'aube," "les édicules sur les caps et les croix aux carrefours," "leurs couches soyeuses," "tout cet attouchment," "s'en furent aux feux," "poussière et poudre de pollen," "dans le vent ne lèvent pas en vain le fouet," "murs polis par le silence et par la science," "chante à l'antiphonaire de typhons," "Et toi, douceur, qui vas mourir, couvre-toi la face de ta toge."

The poet anticipates the future after the wind has completed its task: "Ah! oui, toutes choses descellées! Qu'on se le dise entre vivants!" "Ha! oui, toutes choses descellées, ha! oui, toutes choses lacérées! Et l'An qui passe, l'aile haute!" Intimations of the future are seen in the repeated use of "vin nouveau" and "hommes nouveaux" as well as in the alliterative line, "Vous qui savez, rives futures, où s'éveilleront nos actes, et dans quelles chairs nouvelles se lèveront nos dieux, gardez-nous un lit pur de toute défaillance. . . ."

Although Terpsichore opens the first ode, "Les Muses" is dedicated to Mnémosyne. Metaphorically, Claudel characterizes memory as being a "trésor jaillissant," the interior sense of the spirit, the interior hour, the spiritual weight, and the enclosed source. It is through a silent interiorization—"dans le silence du silence Mnémosyne soupire"—that the poet's creative forces are set in motion. Of this spiritual state he says, "Je suis initié au silence." Ideas are born which create the necessary mode of expression for the evocation of the desired image. Each image is often so connotative that it provokes another. Serialization is maintained by the anaphoric use of "Maintenant," "Soudain," "Puisque," "O," "Et," "Que," and "Car." This seems to account for the many metaphors and especially the analogies which abound in *Cinq Grandes Odes*. On almost every page there are comparisons expressed by "comme," "ainsi que," "pareil(le) à," "de même que," and similar expressions which form series of juxtaposed images.

As he gathers the forces for his poem, Claudel addresses an invocation to his soul: "O mon âme!" "O mon âme sauvage," "O mon âme impatiente, pareille à l'aigle sans art!" After comparing his soul to an eagle, he makes the comparison more important by an enlarged image of the eagle which does not know how to make its nest, and an additional image of the sea eagle which pounces on a fish. The ferocity of the sea eagle's action is such that one sees only a whirlwind of wings and a splashing of foam: ". . . un éclatant tourbillon d'ailes et l'éclaboussement de l'écume!" One can almost hear the splash. The image created by repetition, analogy, and alliteration shows that the poet wants to avoid a sterile composition limited by canons and conventions. He wants to create a poem that is as wild and free as his poetic spirit.

The idea of freedom is echoed in this optative and repetitive line: "Que je ne sache point ce que je dis! que je sois une note en travail! que je sois anéanti dans mon mouvement!" (I, 227). This wish describes the "rapt" recounted in "L'Esprit et l'Eau," the "rapt" which descended upon him after the silence: "Soudain l'Esprit de nouveau, soudain le souffle de nouveau, / Soudain le coup sourd au coeur, soudain le mot donné, soudain le souffle de l'Esprit, le rapt sec, soudain la possession de l'Esprit!" (II, 234). The repetition of "soudain," "souffle," and "Esprit" in this sonorous, alliterative line indicates the intense and passionate experience which makes the poem possible. A sudden inspiration renews the breath of the spirit and enables the poet to find the creative word. After experiencing the "rapt," he exults over his freedom: "Puisque je suis libre! que m'importent vos arrangements cruels? puisque moi du moins je suis libre! puisque j'ai trouvé! puisque moi du moins je suis dehors! / Puisque je n'ai plus ma place avec les choses créées, mais ma part avec ce qui les crée, l'esprit liquide et lascif!" (II, 235). Repetition emphasizes to the poet the importance of his condition.

The creative trance endows the poet with the ability to encompass everything. A triple repetition reveals the scope of the poem: ". . . il y a l'inexhaustible cérémonie vivante, il y a un monde à envahir, il y a un poëme insatiable à remplir. . . ." The importance of space as represented by the sea and the high significance of that which is to be revealed are seen in the following citation and in the typographical disposition of the words on the page:

> Ni
> Le marin, ni
> Le poisson qu'un autre poisson à manger
> Entraîne, mais la chose même et tout le tonneau et la veine vive,
> Et l'eau même, et l'élément même, je joue, je resplendis!
> Je partage la liberté de la mer omniprésente! (II, 236)

The spacing and the overflow of words reflect the emotion and the high purpose of Claudel. After the first "Ni," a full exhalation of the breath is necessary before he can continue. The "coupe" is a common device of the poet which permits an exhalation of the breath after a highly charged utterance before proceeding to the next. "Ni" standing alone represents graphically the splendid nudity of the word spoken of by both Claudel and Perse. The repetition of "même" and alliteration simply intensify the significance of the poem's content.

As in the works of Perse, one finds in the *Odes* of Claudel many references to the sea as the poem. There are many metaphors, analogies, and other devices used to characterize the sea. The ode "L'Esprit et l'Eau" is the sea, the sea of all human words. The sea is life itself: "Mais elle est la vie même sans laquelle tout est mort, ah! je veux la vie même sans laquelle tout est mort!" There is the image of the fertility of the sea in this play on words: "La matière première! C'est la mère, je dis qu'il me faut!" The sea is also "éternelle et salée," "la grande rose grise," "le paradis," "la mer aux entrailles de raisin." At dawn, goddesses play "dans la grande dentelle blanche, dans le feu jaune et froid, dans la mer gazeuze et pétillante." Lace and fire, white, yellow, cold, and sparkling—the sea is everything. There are several coordinate and repetitive expressions in which the work of the sea is compared to that of the spirit, and the poet is himself spirit: "Pas la mer, mais je suis esprit; et comme l'eau / De l'eau, l'esprit reconnaît l'esprit, / L'esprit, le souffle secret, / L'esprit créateur qui fait rire, l'esprit de vie et la grande haleine pneumatique, le dégagement de l'esprit / Qui chatouille et qui enivre et qui fait rire!" "L'Eau / Odore l'eau, et moi je suis plus qu'elle-même liquide." "L'eau qui a fait la terre la délie, l'esprit qui a fait la porte ouvre la serrure." "L'eau / Appréhende l'eau, l'esprit odore l'essence." "Et l'esprit est désirant, mais l'eau est la chose désirée."

The solicitation of Claudel is as insistent as that of Perse as he seeks enlightenment and deliverance from the shadows which engulf him: "O mon Dieu, mon être soupire vers le vôtre! / Délivrez-moi de moi-même! délivrez l'être de la condition! / Je suis libre, délivrez-moi de la liberté!" "Délivrez-moi du temps"; "Libérez-moi de l'esclavage et du poids de cette matière inerte! / Clarifiez-moi donc! dépouillez-moi de ces ténèbres exécrables." In the "Magnificat," the poet shouts his gratitude for deliverance in the repeated phrase, "Soyez béni, mon Dieu."

To a more limited degree yet more intensely than Perse, Claudel comments on the vanity and decadence of past civilizations. Figuratively, the wind also is a destructive force which plays a role in cleansing the earth for its rebirth. The suddenness of the breath of the Spirit which causes the "rapt sec" is that of the wind of Zeus in a whirlwind of straw, dust, and the dirty linen of the whole village, "un tourbillon plein de pailles et de poussières." The old Chinese city stands in the old wind of the earth, the yellow wind, the wind of ashes and of dust, "le grand vent gris qui fut Sodome, et les empires d'Egypte et des Perses, et Paris, et Tadmor, et Babylone." While contemplating the whole of creation, Claudel again speaks of the wind: "Et voici le vent qui se lève à son tour sur la terre, le Semeur, le Moissonneur." The wind's role then extends beyond that of destruction. In an article on *Vents* by Saint-John Perse, Claudel describes the wind as the solemn respiratory function of our world; its breath is sometimes violent, sometimes perfidious, and sometimes meditative.[18] In "La Maison Fermée," he names the four cardinal virtues which stand guard at the portals of his soul. Force, the second of the virtues, stands guard at the south and all winds blow on its face—the south wind like an exhalation from hell, and the summer monsoon from the southwest like a sweating and naked woman: "Le vent du Sud pareil à l'exhalation de l'enfer . . / Et le premier souffle de la mousson d'été, pareil à une femme suante et nue. . . ." All of the analogies and alliterative phrases used to describe the wind are suggestive of its nature by their harshness, sonority, or harmony.

In the *Odes*, there are many instances of antithesis, including the juxtaposition of the vulgar and of the sublime. In a letter to Darius Milhaud, December 17, 1927, Claudel discussed Milhaud's score for *Les Euménides*. In regards to the spoken part of the Oracle, he said that there should be a bond between the spoken word and music since everything is poetry, and that there exists continuity between the most commonplace and the

18. *Oeuvres Complètes* (Paris, 1950–), "Un Poème de Saint-John Perse," Vol. XVIII, *Accompagnements* (1961), p. 239.

most sublime words.[19] The synthesis achieved with contrasts is fundamental in the poetic work of Claudel. Synthesis demonstrates the unity of the created world, the unity of the poem, and the singleness of purpose of the poet. In "L'Esprit et l'Eau" there is "la goutte unique," "la goutte translucide," and "la goutte glorifiée" all of which may be the distillation in the poet's mind of the handiwork of God. In the fourth ode, the Muse tells the poet: "C'est le feu pur et simple qui fait de plusieurs choses une seule."

Among the many kinds of comparisons and contrasts which abound in the *Odes*, the broad range of the disparate is evident in several instances. There is continuity between the greatest Angel and a pebble: "Ainsi du plus grand Ange . . . jusqu'au caillou . . . / Il ne cesse point continuité . . ."; ". . . le corps de gloire désire sous le corps de boue"; the poet who has drunk of the new wine leaps like a naked god on the stage; the human soul is a more precious elixir than the liquefied blueness of the atmosphere; the sun of the spirit is like a grasshopper in the sun of God; the lover's emotion cannot compare with the divine energy of the spirit; the bell-tower in the sun is clearer than wine; the bronze clocks are as pure as lilies; as a man crumbles bread for the birds, so does the poet with the prayers of his rosary nourish the souls in purgatory. As man received the blessings of the first five days of Creation, so will Jacob receive "la bénédiction de l'abîme subjacent, la bénédiction des mamelles et de la vulve, / La bénédiction sur son front sera fortifiée de la bénédiction de ses pères." The twentieth century is hailed as the era of the establishment of the universal church. The souls which make up the church are compared to a net of fish whose scales come alive in the torchlight. The stars resemble grazing sheep and are as numerous as the posterity of Abraham. The suns enfolded in the cold nebula are like larvae enveloped in their satin, padded sacks. Then there is the line which describes the dew as portraying the sanctity of the body and soul: "Si la rosée rutile dans le soleil, / Combien plus l'escarboucle humaine et l'âme substantielle dans le rayon intelligible."

19. *Cahiers Paul Claudel* (Paris, 1959–), Vol. III, *Correspondance Paul Claudel-Darius Milhaud* (1961), p .86.

One finds in Claudel an abundance of anacolutha and convoluted sentences: "Et je tends les mains à gauche et à droite / Afin qu'aucune par moi / Lacune dans la parfaite enceinte qui est de vos Créatures existe!" This statement indicates the solidarity and unity of man and the universe, and the poet envelops the totality within the poem. The poet seems overwhelmed by the magnitude of Creation in this redundant statement: "Mais ici et où que je tourne le visage et de cet autre côté / Il y en a plus et encore et là aussi et toujours et de même et davantage! Toujours, cher coeur!" The string of adverbs is a sort of continuity resembling that which the poet envisages in the structure of the universe.

There are other common characteristics with slight variations in the works of both poets which have not been mentioned, and which may provide a point of departure for another study. Among these is the use of the familiar "tu" and its corresponding forms. These forms occur for the most part when the poets are communing with themselves in a meditative interior dialogue. Particularly, the forms occur in instances of personification, in invocations, and in soliloquies. One finds also in the poems some humor or buffoonery, a simulation perhaps on the human level of "le rire divin." The latter is not humorous; rather it is the lyrical expression of joy at the moment of inspiration. "La Muse qui est la Grâce" invites Claudel to share in the joy of creation. There is humor as such when the Muse reprimands him for his obstinacy while addressing him as "pataud aux larges pieds," "lourd imbécile," "sot," "tête de pierre," and "face d'âne." Except for the lyrical descriptions of the splendor of the universe and the passionate joy of love, the laughter or smile of Perse is more of a grimace as he contemplates and describes the ways and the professions of man.

The examples chosen from the poems of Claudel and Perse, though not exhaustive, illustrate their mastery of prosodic technique and represent the diverse character of their work. The kinds of devices used determine what Claudel calls the texture of language and thought. The principal device utilized in the creation of the texture is the metaphor, formed by rhetoric from a rapport among things, people, and ideas. This rapport con

stitutes the analogy.[20] The poems of both poets are multi-
textured because of the richness of language and the images cre-
ated by analogies and metaphors. Various critics have charac-
terized their work, as to language and total effect, as dignified,
dramatic, lyrical, and symphonic. Dignity in the poems derives
from the poets' concern with such fundamental themes as the
origin and purpose of the universe, the universals of humanity,
the condition of mankind and his destiny. The consideration
of such themes calls for an elevated tone which in Claudel often
verges on the sublime. One could scarcely apply the term
"sublime" to Perse because of his concentration on the mundane
in his search for answers.

Perse is perhaps more dramatic than Claudel, particularly in
Amers. There one finds the skeletal structure of the ancient
Greek drama with its "strophe" and "choeur." In a letter to
a Swedish writer, Perse speaks of the sea as the solitary arena,
the ritual center, "l'aire théâtrale," and the altar table of ancient
drama around which unfolds the action.[21] After the exposition
or prologue in the "Invocation," the dramatic element evolves in
the presentation of the tragic condition of mankind. The resolu-
tion of this condition will come about through a communion of
minds and love. A dramatic component equally as important as
that of the status of mankind is the poet's encounter with him-
self in his confrontation with a silent and hostile universe. The
resolution of this dilemma is perceived when he, in a state of
exaltation, acknowledges and reveals the hidden cosmic mean-
ing in every visible aspect of the universe. The sense of drama
is amplified by eloquent and elevated language, monologues, and
soliloquies.

The *Cinq Grandes Odes* are also dramatic in their presenta-
tion of universal and personal discord. The five odes could real-
ly be compared to the five acts of a drama. The resolution of
universal disorder will occur in the envisioned solidarity of man-
kind and the communion of souls. For Claudel as well as for
mankind this depends upon a return to the source, God. The

20. *Oeuvres Complètes,* "La Poésie est un Art," Vol. XVIII, *Accom-
pagnements* (1961), p. 19.
21. "La Thématique d'*Amers*," *Honneur à Saint-John Perse* (Paris,
1965), p. 665.

personal confrontation of Claudel with himself occurs particularly in the fourth ode. This he has structured into strophe and antistrophe which is the dialogue between himself and the "Muse qui est la Grâce." The ode ends with the epode in which the poet refuses to yield to the Muse. In the fifth ode, his soul becomes a closed circle, "La Maison Fermée," a tabernacle for God.

Both poets become lyrical in their contemplation of splendor and in their anticipation of joy. The emotion which they experience at the moment of "rapt" expands their sensitivity. In an almost Rimbaldian condition, short of the hallucinatory state, they see and hear colors, touch and smell sounds, taste odors, and intuit an invisible cosmic essence. The expression of this experience is ordered and disordered, but the total effect is one of musicality because of the internal rhythms, harmonious chords, and central theme. It is for this reason perhaps that one cannot really explain or interpret the poems of Claudel and Perse. They must be read and experienced in the same manner that one would listen to a symphony or contemplate a work of art.

Claudel and Perse, like Boris Pasternak's man, had a "longing to grasp and experience and express everything in the world." As an explorer of the Universe, Claudel confirmed his belief that God is the Source. Perse, in his quest for the Source, seemed to have found it even as he elaborated on its elusiveness and ineffability.

Appendix,
Bibliography, and Index

Appendix

✦

Translation of French Passages in the Text

page 6 (*Art Poétique*, p. 184)

In relation to the world, he is charged with the rôle of origin, with 'making' the principle according to which everything is ordered . . . he is the general, he is the seal of authenticity. In relation to God, he is the delegate for external affairs, the *representative* and the envoy with power of attorney.

page 6 (Murciaux, *Saint-John Perse*, pp. 56–57)

The proselytism of Claudel came near foundering this friend-ship; Saint-John Perse . . . was upset to the point of weeping because of the imperious eloquence of Claudel. Nevertheless he was not converted by this 'too cruel' man.

page 7 (*Poésie*, pp. 14–15)

For, if poetry is not itself, as some have claimed, 'absolute reality,' it is poetry which shows the strongest passion for and the keenest apprehension of it, to that extreme limit of com-plicity where reality seems to shape itself within the poem.

CHAPTER II

page 9 (*Mémoires Improvisés*, p. 24)

> The cause to a large extent of my lack of orientation was the heavy boredom which accompanied my transfer from a small provincial town in which, in short, I was perfectly happy with my family, to Paris, where the atmosphere was completely different. I had to adapt myself to it, and this adaptation, which has never been complete, was very painful.

page 10 (Mondor, *Claudel plus intime*, p. 37)

> The nostalgic longing for his native town by this recently uprooted person, so unhappy with Paris, must have been particularly stirring, almost tormenting, for nowhere in the later work, not even in *La Jeune Fille Violaine*, will occur the experience of agricultural life with so much prolixity and exuberance....

page 10 (I, 63)

> O Despoiled! / You wept to remember the surf in the moonlight; the whistlings of the more distant shores; the strange music that is born and is muffled under the folded wing of the night, / like the linked circles that are the waves of a conch, or the amplifications of the clamours under the sea ...

page 11 (I, 23)

> I remember the tears on a day too beautiful in too much fright, in too much fright! ... and the white sky, O silence! which flamed like a fevered gaze ... I weep, how I weep in the hollow of old gentle hands ... / Oh! it is a pure sob that will not be comforted, oh! it is only that, already rocking my forehead like a big morning star.

CHAPTER III

page 15 (*Art Poétique*, p. 190)

> Each man has been created to be the witness and the actor of a certain spectacle in order to determine for himself the meaning of it.

page 16 (III, 249)

> You have called me by my name / As someone who knows it, you have chosen me among all of my contemporaries.

page 17 (III, 261)

> For what is any prize and enjoyment and property and arrangement / In comparison with the intelligence of the poet who makes of several things together a single thing with him / Since to understand is to remake / The thing itself that one has grasped with oneself.

page 17 (*Oeuvres Complètes*, XVIII, 239)

And yet, led by the sun to the reverse side of this sometimes violent, and sometimes perfidious, and sometimes meditative breath, what was he going to search for beyond every barrier, what was he going to demand from the reservoirs of the incommensurable?

page 18 (*Poésie*, p. 16)

Refusing to divorce art from life or love from knowledge, it is action, it is passion, it is power . . . In one embrace, as in one great living strophe, it gathers to its present all the past and the future, the human and the superhuman, planetary space and total space.

page 19 (II, 246)

My God, / I see myself and I judge myself, and I no longer have any value for myself. / You have given me life: I give it back to you; I prefer that you take back everything. / I finally see myself! and I am grieved by it, and the sorrow within me opens everything like a liquid eye. / O my God, I no longer want anything, and I give you back all, and nothing has any more value for me, / And I see no more than my misery, and my nothingness, and my deprivation, and that at least is mine!

page 19 (IV, 275)

Liberate yourself! Unifier of all men, unify yourself! / Be a single spirit! be a single purpose!

page 20 (I, 94)

You are the Healer and the Assessor and the Enchanter at the sources of the spirit! For your power over the hearts of men is a strange thing and great is your ease among us. / I have seen the sign on your forehead and I have considered what your role is among us.

page 20 (II, 202)

For us the Continent of the sea, not the nuptial land with its perfume of fenugreek; for us the free space of the sea, not this earthly side of man, blinded by domestic stars.

page 21 (I, 172–73)

Honour thine exile, O Prince! / And all at once all is power and presence for me, here where the theme of nothingness rises still in smoke.

page 21 (II, 31–32)

O you whom the storm refreshes . . . freshness and promise of freshness . . . / Your countenance recovered from the gods, your radiance from the fire of the forges, / Behold, you take your stand on this side of the Century, where you followed your calling. / . . . And if the man of talent prefers the rose-garden and the playing of the harpsichord, he shall be devoured by the dogs.

page 21 (II, 77)

For man is in question, in his human presence; and the eye's enlargement over the loftiest inner seas. / Make haste! make haste! testimony for man!

page 22 (II, 80)

. . . With his tribe of attendants, with his tribe of followers, and all his train of rags in the wind, O smile, O gentleness, / The Poet himself at the gangway of the Century!—Welcome on the causeway of men, and the wind bending the new grass a hundred leagues away. / For man is in question, and his reintegration. / Will no one in the world raise his voice? Testimony for man . . . / Let the poet speak, and let him guide the judgment!

page 23 (IV, 264)

What do all men matter to me at present! It is not for them that I am made, but for the / Transport of this sacred meter!

page 23 (IV, 269)

Fie upon you, O contemptible terrestrial days! O nuptials! O premises of the spirit! drink only of this unfermented wine! / Advance and see the eternal morning, the land and the sea under the morning sun, like someone who appears before the throne of God!

page 23 (IV, 275)

. . . it is I who chose you before you were born. / Among all living beings, I am the word of grace addressed to you alone.

CHAPTER IV

page 27 (II, 15)

Divination by rain . . . / And such rites were favourable. I shall make use of them. Favour of the god on my poem! And never from my poem be it withdrawn! / 'Favoured by the favourable dream' was the phrase chosen to exalt the condition of the sage. And once again the poet receives grace from his poem.

page 27 (p. 234)

Suddenly the Spirit again, suddenly the breath again, / Suddenly the muffled blow to the heart, suddenly the word given, suddenly the breath of the Spirit, the sharp rape, Suddenly the possession of the Spirit!

page 28 (II, 82)

Let them not say: Sadness. . . revelling in it—say: Sadness . . . lingering in it, as though in the alcoves of love. / Injunction against living on it! Injunction made to the poet, made to the spinners of memory.

page 28 (II, 83)

I shall liquidate you, logic, on whose shackles our beasts disabled themselves.

page 28 (II, 82)

Blur yourself, clear eye, in which the man of reason placed his trust.

page 28 (II, 28)

Others have drunk the new wine in fountains painted with red lead. And we were of those. And may the sadness that we were be dissolved in the new wine of men, as in the festivals of the wind!

page 31 (II, 235)

But what do your empires matter to me at present, and all that which dies, / And the rest of you whom I have left, your hideous road over there! / Since I am free! what do your cruel arrangements matter to me? since I at least I am free! since I have found! since I at least I am outside! / Since I no longer have my place with created things, but my part with that which creates them, the liquid and lascivious spirit!

page 31 (*Présence et Prophétie*, p. 250)

Does not one say of the spirit that it moves, that it flies, that it soars, that it flashes, that it gains step by step information . . . ?

page 32 (II, 242–43)

Thus the voice with which I make eternal words about you! I can name nothing except the eternal. / The leaf yellows and the fruit falls, but the leaf in my verses does not perish, / Neither the ripe fruit, nor the rose among roses! / It perishes, but its name in the spirit which is my spirit no longer perishes.

CHAPTER V

page 35 (I, 171–72)

. . . There has always been this clamour, there has always been this grandeur, / This thing wandering about the world, and on all the shores of the world, by the same breath uttered,

the same wave uttering / One long phrase without pause for-
ever unintelligible . . .

page 36 (II, 46)

Lifting a finger of flesh in the rush of the wind, I question,
O Power! And you, take note that my query is not common-
place. / For the exigency within us was extreme* [great] . . . /
And still my face is in the wind.

* *extrème*, 1946 edition; *grande*, 1960 edition of *Oeuvre Poétique*.

page 36 (I, 105)

. . . the thorn to your flesh; the very point of the spirit's sword.
The bee of language is on their brow. / And on the heavy
human phrase, kneaded with so many idioms, they are the
only ones to wield the sling of the accent.

page 38 (II, 121)

When violence had remade the bed of men on the earth, /
A very old tree, barren of leaves, resumed the thread of its
maxims . . . / And another tree of high degree was already
rising from the great subterranean Indies, / With its magnetic
leaf and its burden of new fruits.

page 38 (II, 39–40)

. . . New lands, out there, in their very lofty perfume of humus
and foliage, / New lands, out there, beneath the lengthening
of this world's most expansive shadows, / . . . New lands,
up there, like a powerful perfume of tall women ripening . . . /
All the land of trees, up there, in the swaying of its most
beautiful shades, opening the blackest of its tresses and the
imposing ornament of its plumage, like a perfume of flesh,
nubile and vigorous, in the bed of this world's most beautiful
beings.

page 39 (II, 34)

Eâ, god of the abyss, the temptations of doubt would be
prompt / Were the wind to fail . . . But the fever of the soul
prevails, / And contrary to the solicitations of doubt, may
the demands of the soul on the flesh / Keep us breathless,
and the wing of the Wind be with us!

page 40 (*Poésie*, p. 15)

. . . it is the poetic image which rekindles the high passion of
mankind in its quest for light.

page 40 (II, 73)

For our quest is no longer for copper or virgin gold, no
longer for coal or naphtha, but like the germ itself beneath
its arch in the apses of life, and like the blast itself beneath
the lightning in the caverns of the Seer, we seek, in the kernel

and the ovule and the core of new species, at the hearth of the force the very spark of its cry!

page 40 (II, 76)

You shall reveal yourself, new cipher: in the diagrams of stone and the atom's indices; / At the great forbidden tables where the signs more swiftly pass . . .

page 41 (II, 92)

If living is like this, let us seize upon it! Ah! let us force it, / With one and the same blast in the wind, with one and the same wave on its course, / To its limit!

page 41 (II, 93–94)

Tall girls were given us, who unwound in their bridal arms more hydras than did our flights. / Where are you who were there, silent aroma of our nights, O chaste ones setting free in your wanton hair an ardent history of living beings? / You who will hear us one night at the turn of these pages, on the storm's last scatterings, Faithful Ones with ospreys' eyes, you will know that with you, / One night we took once more the road of human beings.

page 42 (II, 113)

Let them sluice out all of that! Let them slice for us that loaf of garbage and mucus. And all that sediment of the ages on their phlegm!

page 43 (II, 70)

But their quest was for no more than gold and grants . . . / Buzzards on the passes, caught at the curve of their soaring, enlarged the circle and measure of human possession.

page 44 (II, 70, 71)

And then came the men of barter and trade. Men of wide range gloved with buff leather for abuse. And all the men of justice, assemblers of police and leviers of militia. The Governors in plum purple and their russet-fleshed daughters smelling of ferrets. / And then the people of the Papacy in search of great Vicarates; the Chaplains in the saddle and dreaming, at evening's fall, of fine straw-yellow dioceses with hemicycles of pink stone . . .

page 44 (II, 119, 120)

And you can replace in the fire the great blades, colour of liver under oil. We shall make of them iron for the plough, we shall know again the earth open to love, the earth moving, under love, with a movement heavier than pitch. . . . / A new race among the men of my race, a new race among the daughters of my race.

page 45 (II, 228)

. . . you are no Virgin raised from the depths, Victory of bronze or white stone recovered, with the amphora . . .

page 46 (II, 236)

You are the idol of virgin copper, in the form of a fish, that is smeared with honey from the rocks and the cliffs . . . You are the sea itself in its lustre, when noon, explosive and violent, spills the oil of its lamps.

page 46 (II, 232)

For you night opens a woman: her body, her havens, her shore; and her primeval night where all memory lies.

page 47 (II, 240–41)

But tongue to tongue, and breath to breath, panting, her face streaming and her eyes devoured with acid, she who alone sustains the ardent controversy, the Lover, erect in wrath, who recoils, who bends taut, and stands fast, utters her hissing of lover and priestess . . . / Will you strike, divine staff? . . . / You will strike, promise! . . . / Speak louder, despot! and assail me more assiduously: irritation is at its height. Search farther, royal Conger: so does lightning on the sea seek the ship for a sheath . . . / You have struck, divine lightning! Who in me gives this very great cry of a woman unweaned? . . . O splendour! O sadness! and the very tall comb of immortality crowning the radiant foam! and all this glory which flares out, golden harrow! . . . Did I haunt there the forbidden, and the heart of fable?

page 47 (II, 238)

One same wave throughout the world, one same wave our course . . . Narrow the measure, narrow the caesura, which breaks the woman's body at the middle like an ancient metre.

page 47 (II, 269)

And the woman is in the man, and in the man is the sea, and love sails far from death on all the seas.

page 48 (II, 290)

And you will be with us against the night of men . . . / We cross at last the royal green of the threshold; and doing more than dream of you, we walk in you, divine fable!

page 49 (II, 141)

. . . a crowd in haste rising on the tiers of History and all moving in a body towards the arena, with the first chill of the evening and the smell of seaweed, / Recitation marching towards the Author and towards the painted mouth of his mask.

page 49 (II, 133)

The Sea, in us bearing the silken sound of open seas and all the great freshness of good fortune throughout the world.

CHAPTER VI

page 50 (*Figures et Paraboles*, pp. 152–53)

He made everything. He created everything. But He created everything in order and in charity, making use of that which was before in order to bring about that which is after, utilizing accordingly the means which he originated, and among them this spontaneity, this inventive, productive, and reproductive capacity of nature, the response from this void which He inflated with His breath.

page 51 (*Figures et Paraboles*, p. 110)

God by giving us conscience, opened to us an eye not only on the depths of ourselves, but on all the interior forces of production and development of this world which He has made. We have only to look within ourselves to find laid out there the Earth, the Sea, the starry Sky . . .

page 51 (V, 282)

Not one thing which is not necessary to the others.

page 53 (II, 235)

Behold the Ode, behold this great new Ode is presented to you, / Not at all as a thing which begins, but by degrees as the sea which was there, / The sea of all human words . . .

page 53 (II, 243)

God who breathed on chaos . . . / You command likewise my waters, you have put in my nostrils the same spirit of creation and of form.

page 53 (*Partage*, I, 931)

He lives, I live; he thinks and I weigh in my heart his thought. / He who made my eyes, can I not see him at all? himself who made my heart.

page 53 (*Partage*, I, 931)

I who loved so much these visible things, O I would have wished to see, to have with appropriation, / Not at all only with my eyes, or only my senses, but with the intelligence of the spirit / And to know everything in order to be completely known.

page 54 (*Art Poétique*, 202)

There is a harmony, at each moment of duration among all parts of creation, from the Seraph to the worm.

page 54 (*Partage*, I, 957)

And passionately I feel beneath me you who abjure, and in me the profound disturbance / of creation, like the Earth / When with foam on her lips produced the arid thing, and in a frightful contraction / She thrust forth her substance and the double fold of the mountains like paste!

page 55 (II, 238)

As the tree in the new spring-time each year / Invents, Obsessed by its soul, / The green, the same which is eternal, creates from nothing its pointed leaf, / I, man, / I know what I am doing, / Of the thrust and of this same power of birth and of creation / I make use, I am master, / I am in the world, I exert on all sides my knowledge. / I know all things and all things know each other in me. / I bring to everything its deliverance.

page 55 (V, 289)

We have conquered the world and we have found that Your Creation is complete / And that the imperfect has no place at all with your completed works, and that our imagination cannot add / A single figure to this Number in ecstasy before Your Unity.

page 55 (II, 240)

It is closed by your will as by a wall and by your power as by a very strong enclosure!

page 56 (*Soulier de Satin*, II, 727–28)

This Nothingness on the edge of which they have been seated for such a long time, this Void left by the absence of the Being, where plays the reflection of Heaven, it was necessary to bring God to them in order that they may understand it completely.

page 56 (*Soulier*, II, 773)

It is because I am a catholic man, it is in order that all parts of humanity may be reunited and that there be none which believes it has the right to live in its heresy, / Separated from all the others as if they were not in need of it. . . . You will no longer be alone! I bring you the world, the total word of God, all of these brothers whether it pleases you or not to learn about them, all of these brothers from a single source.

page 57 (*Oeuvre Poétique*, 300)
Behold the multitude of all of my brothers living and dead, / the unanimity of the catholic people . . .

page 57 (*Soulier*, II, 772)
Why the endless wind which torments me? says the pine. To what is it so necessary to cling? What dies thus in ecstasy? says the chrysanthemum.—What is there so black that I may exist, a cypress?—What does one call the azure that I may be so blue?—What exists so sweet that I may be so rosy? . . . How strong a thing the water is that it has made me merit this bit of a tail and this jacket of scales!—Of what ruin, says the rock, am I the debris? For what absent inscription is my flank prepared?

page 58 (*La Messe*, 500)
If the world did not speak of You so much, my ennui would not be such.

page 58 (*Soulier*, II, 691–92)
What matters the disorder, and today's sorrow since it is the beginning of something else, since / Tomorrow exists, since life continues, this demolition with us of the immense reserves of creation, / Since the hand of God has not ceased its movement which writes with us in long and short lines on eternity, / Down to the commas, down to the most imperceptible period, / This book which will have no meaning until it is finished. . . . Of all of these scattered movements, I know quite well that there is being prepared an accord, since they are already united enough to be discordant.

page 59 (IV, 267)
And I say that there is nothing in nature which is made without design and purpose addressed to man, / And as light for the eye and sound for the ear, thus everything for analysis by the intelligence . . .

page 60 (*Soulier*, II, 723)
And what more powerful flesh to speak to man than that of woman?

page 60 (*Partage*, I, 934)
It is hard to keep all of one's heart. It is hard not to be loved. It is hard to be alone. It is hard to wait, / and to endure, and to wait, and to wait always . . .

page 61 ("Les Grandes Odes de Claudel," pp. 166–67)
It suffices for these two beings to touch each other for the great human flame to burst forth.

page 61 (*Oeuvre Poétique*, 313–18)

'Tis thee: / . . . Below thy bosom, mortal Mistress mine / Immortal by my kiss, / Leaps what sweet pain?. . . . Himself the God let blame / If all about him bursts to quenchless flame!. . . . O, too much joy; O, touch of airy fire; O, turmoil of content; O, unperturb'd desire, / From founts of spirit impell'd through brain and blood!

page 62 (*Partage*, 987)

. . . in an interpenetration / Inexpressible, in the voluptuousness of the conjugal difference, man and woman like two great spiritual animals.

page 62 (III, 258)

God be praised because I no longer remain unique, / And that from me life has come forth . . . and that from me in my turn, in this image forever real, of a soul joined with a body, / You have received form and dimension.

page 62 (*Soulier*, II, 681–82)

If I cannot be his paradise, at least I can be his cross! So that his soul with his body may be quartered on it I am quite equal to these two pieces of wood which cross each other! / Since I cannot give him heaven, at least I can uproot him from the earth. I alone can furnish him an insufficiency to the measure of his desire! . . . . He asked a woman for God and she was capable of giving Him to him, for there is nothing in heaven or earth that love is not capable of giving!

page 65 (III, 257)

Be praised, my God, who delivered me from myself, / and who causes me not to place my well-being in myself . . . / But in your will alone, / And not in any wealth, but in your will alone.

page 66 (*Théâtre*, I, 180)

All diseases attend us, ulcer and abcess, epilepsy and the shaking of the head, and at the end comes the gout and the gravel which prevents urination. / Consumption creates its fire; the secret parts grow moldy like grapes; and the sac of the belly / Bursts and empties outside entrails and excrement! / Is it not horrible? but our life / Which becomes a festival stuffing itself on a repast of larva, / Until, like a dog which vomits worms and bits of meat, / The crammed belly revolts and throws up on the table!

page 66 (*Théâtre*, I, 437)

. . . the last sleep of the sick who has also finished suffering . . .

page 66 (*Cantate*, 334–35)

It is reality which blooms an instant for us beneath these fragile veils . . . / Ah, how fragile is this instant in the middle of the year . . . !

page 66 (*Art Poétique*, 184)

Properly human then is what I shall call sentiment of the stem; the sentiment of origin, the religious sentiment (*religare*), the mysterious placental attachment.

page 67 (*Oeuvre Poétique*, 465–66)

Do you find it worthy of you to follow me thus? / Spying on the thing that I am going to do . . . / I who will be destroyed in a moment like a garment eaten by cockroaches! . . . And it is true that my sins are great . . . / Leave me at peace a moment, remove Yourself from me a little while / Time for me to swallow my saliva! / . . . Listen to the cry of Your little ones who are killed and the silence of the guiltless child . . . / That makes no difference, O my God, and I do know that it is not Your fault! . . . And even if You were to damn me, I know that you are my Creator! / You are my Father just the same!

CHAPTER VII

page 70 (*Art Poétique*, 134)

What then is this force deprived of a source, this machine which nourishes itself and produces itself? Plaything, which is in motion, without any purpose except its very movement, by the single incapacity to stop itself. Here is the eternal automaton dancing indefinitely!

page 75 (*Art Poétique*, p. 132)

. . . man is still naked! Beneath the unclean garment, he is pure as a stone!

page 76 (II, 232)

Does the night through which you steer hold no island, no shore? Who then in you always becomes estranged and denies himself?

page 77 (*Chronique*, II, 328)

. . . do we really know toward what species we are advancing?

page 77 (II, 324)

O death . . . you cross in vain our paths cobbled with bones, for our way lies beyond . . . / . . . we live on what is beyond death, and on death itself shall we live.

page 78 (p. 429)
> . . . consummate mimic / Penetrating by imitation the most
> secret movements of nature, / You make them serve human
> uses.

CHAPTER VIII

page 81 (V, 278)
> Is it the language of a man or of some animal? . . . / But you
> twist and mix together everything in the surf of your inter-
> mingled lines . . .

page 82 (*Positions et Propositions*, I, 60)
> What is to be done . . . to keep this freedom, this ease, this
> liveliness, this sparkle of the spoken language, and yet give
> it this consistency and this inner organization which inscrip-
> tion on paper demands? How does one open to the Muse a
> pathway of roses? how intoxicate it without ever surfeiting
> it with a music which has at the same time the interest of
> research and the calmness of authority? how does one keep
> the dream while dispelling sleep? How sustain its pace with
> a harmony at once perceptible and unfathomable as the heart?

page 85 (II, 86)
> Not the writing, but the thing itself. Seized at the quick
> and in its entirety. / Conservation, not of copies, but of the
> original.

page 86 (II, 307–8)
> And words for us they are no longer, being no longer signs
> or adornments, / But the thing itself which they signify and
> the thing itself they adorned . . .

page 87 (II, 141)
> . . . a language . . . whose phrasing is new . . . / great swellings
> of language, with great reliefs of images and luminous slopes
> of shadow, running to its massive splendours of a very fine
> periodic style . . .

page 88 (II, 296–97)
> Prolific the image, and the metre, prodigal . . . / And mesh
> to mesh is repeated the immense web of poetry.

page 88 (II, 305)
> Sea innumerable in her numbers and her multiple of numbers.

page 88 (II, 310)
> Uterine Sea of our dreams and Sea haunted by the true dream.

page 97 (I, 227)
> May I not know what I am saying! may I be a note in labor!
> may I be annihilated in my movement.

page 97 (II, 236)
> Neither / The sailor, nor / The fish that another fish in order
> to eat / Drags away, but the thing itself and the whole tun
> and the live vein, / And the water itself, and the element it-
> self, I gambol, I glitter! I share the freedom of the omnipresent
> sea!

Selected Bibliography

I. EDITIONS OF CLAUDEL'S WORKS USED IN THIS STUDY

Cahiers Paul Claudel. Vol. I. *"Tête d'Or" et les débuts littéraires*. 5th ed. Paris: Gallimard, 1959. Vol. II. *Le Rire de Paul Claudel*. 1960. Vol. III. *Correspondance Paul Claudel-Darius Milhaud, 1912–1953*. 1961.

Claudel, Paul. *Contacts et Circonstances*. 14th ed. Paris: Gallimard, 1947.

———. *Figures et Paraboles*. 25th ed. Paris: Gallimard, 1936.

———. *Mémoires Improvisés*. Compiled by Jean Amrouche. Paris: Gallimard, 1954.

———. *Oeuvres Complètes*. In process of publication. Paris: Gallimard, 1950–.

———. *Oeuvre Poétique*. Bibliothèque de la Pléiade. Paris: Gallimard, 1957.

———. *Un Poète Regarde la Croix*. 36th ed. Paris: Gallimard, 1935.

———. *Positions et Propositions*. 2 vols. 44th ed. Paris: Gallimard, 1928–1934.

———. *Théâtre*. 2 vols. Bibliothèque de la Pléiade. Paris: Gallimard, 1947–1948.

———, Jammes, Francis, and Frizeau, Gabriel. *Correspondance 1897–1938*. 2d ed. Paris: Gallimard, 1952.

Rivière, Jacques, and Claudel, Paul. *Correspondance, 1907–1914.* Paris: Librairie Plon, 1926.

II. CRITICAL WORKS: BOOKS

Angers, Pierre. *Commentaire à l'Art Poétique de Paul Claudel, avec le texte de l'Art Poétique.* Paris: Mercure de France, 1949.
Antoine, Gerald. *Les Cinq Grandes Odes de Claudel ou la poésie de la répétition.* Paris: Lettres Modernes, 1959.
Barjon, Louis. *Paul Claudel.* Preface by Paul Claudel. Paris: Editions Universitaires, 1953.
Cahiers de la Compagnie Madeleine Renaud–Jean-Louis Barrault. Vol. I. *Paul Claudel et "Christophe Colomb."* Paris: René Julliard, 1953.
Daniel-Rops, Henry. *Claudel tel que je l'ai connu.* Strasbourg–Paris: Editions F. -X Le Roux, 1957.
Fowlie, Wallace. *Climate of Violence: The French Literary Tradition from Baudelaire to the Present.* New York: Macmillan Co.; London: Collier-Macmillan, 1967.
Friche, Ernest. *Etudes Claudéliennes.* Porrentruy: Editions des Portes de France, 1943.
Fumet, Stanislas. *Claudel.* Paris: Gallimard, 1958.
Guillemin, Henri. *Claudel et Son Art d'Ecrire.* 6th ed. Paris: Gallimard, 1955.
Madaule, Jacques. *Le Drame de Paul Claudel.* Preface by Paul Claudel. 4th ed. Paris: Desclée de Brouwer, 1947.
―――. *Reconnaissances.* Vol. I. *Claudel, Proust, DuBos.* Paris: Desclée de Brouwer, 1943. Vol. II. *Un Poète Regarde la Croix.* 1946.
Maritain, Jacques. *Frontières de la Poésie et Autres Essais.* Paris: Louis Rouart et Fils, 1935.
Molitor, André. *Aspects de Paul Claudel.* Paris: Desclée de Brouwer, 1945.
Mondor, Henri. *Claudel Plus Intime.* Paris: Gallimard, 1960.
Perche, Louis. *Paul Claudel.* Paris: Seghers, 1952.
Rivière, Jacques. *Etudes.* 9th ed. Paris: Gallimard, 1924.
Tonquédec, Joseph de. *L'Oeuvre de Paul Claudel.* 3rd ed. Paris: G. Beauchesne, 1927.
Vigée, Claude. *Révoltes et Louanges: Essais sur la poésie moderne.* Paris: Librairie José Corti, 1962.

III. CRITICAL WORKS: PERIODICALS

Fowlie, Wallace. "Claudel: The Tidings that are the Poem." *Poetry,* 87, no. 3 (December 1955), 169–75.
―――. "Vocation of the Poet." *Commonweal,* 62, no. 8 (May 1955), 199–201.

Hommage à Paul Claudel, La Nouvelle Nouvelle Revue Française, III, no. 33 (September 1, 1955), 387–640.

Lorigiola, P., S. J. "Les Grandes Odes de Claudel." *Les Etudes Classiques*, XXVII, no. 2 (April 1959), 152–73; no. 3 (July 1959), 273–92; no. 4 (October 1959), 382–406; XXVIII, no. 1 (January 1960), 30–50.

Manship, J. P. "The Universal Artist." *Commonweal*, 62, no. 8 (May 1955), 201–3.

Turnell, Martin. "The Intolerance of Genius." *Commonweal*, 62, no. 8 (May 1955), 204–6.

IV. EDITIONS OF PERSE'S WORKS USED IN THIS STUDY

Perse, Saint-John. *Oeuvre Poétique*. Vol. I. *Eloges, La Gloire des rois, Anabase, Exil*. Edition rev. and corr. Paris: Gallimard, 1960. Vol. II. *Vents, Amers, Chronique*. Edition rev. and corr. 1960.
———. *Oiseaux*. Paris: Gallimard, 1963.

V. ENGLISH TRANSLATIONS OF PERSE'S WORKS

Anabasis. Translated by T. S. Eliot. Bilingual ed.; rev. and corr. ed. New York: Harcourt, Brace, 1949.

Chronique. Translated by Robert Fitzgerald. Bollingen Series 69. Bilingual ed. New York: Pantheon Books, 1961.

Eloges and Other Poems. Translated by Louise Varèse. Bollingen Series 55. Bilingual ed., rev. New York: Pantheon Books, 1956.

Exile and Other Poems. Translated by Denis Devlin. Bollingen Series 15. Bilingual ed.; 2nd ed. New York: Pantheon Books, 1962.

On Poetry. Translated by W. H. Auden. Bollingen Series. Bilingual ed. New York: Bollingen Foundation, 1961.

Seamarks. Translated by Wallace Fowlie. Bollingen Series 67. Bilingual ed. New York: Pantheon Books, 1958; Harper Torchbooks and Bollingen Library eds., 1961.

Winds. Translated by Hugh Chisolm. Bollingen Series 34. Bilingual ed.; 2nd ed. New York: Pantheon Books, 1961.

VI. CRITICAL WORKS: BOOKS

Bosquet, Alain. *Saint-John Perse*. Paris: Seghers, 1953.

Caillois, Roger. *Poétique de Saint-John Perse*. Paris: Gallimard, 1954.

Charpier, Jacques. *Saint-John Perse*. Paris: Gallimard, 1962.

Fowlie, Wallace. *Climate of Violence: The French Literary Tradition from Baudelaire to the Present*. New York: Macmillan Co.; London: Collier-Macmillan, 1967.

Honneur à Saint-John Perse: Hommages et témoignages littéraires. Paris: Gallimard, 1965.

Murciaux, Christian. *Saint-John Perse*. Paris: Editions Universitaires, 1960.

Parent, Monique. *Saint-John Perse et quelques devanciers: Etudes sur le poème en prose*. Paris: Klincksiek, 1960.

Saillet, Maurice. *Saint-John Perse, poète de gloire*. Paris: Mercure de France, 1952.

Vigée, Claude. *Révolte et Louanges: Essais sur la poésie moderne*. Paris: Librairie José Corti, 1962.

VII. CRITICAL WORKS: PERIODICALS

Caillois, Roger. "The Art of Saint-John Perse," translated by Haakon M. Chevalier. *Sewanee Review*, 53 (Spring 1945), 198–206.

Fowlie, Wallace. "A Note on Saint-John Perse." *Poetry*, 74, no. 6 (September 1949), 343–48.

———. "The Poetics of Saint-John Perse." *Poetry*, 82, no. 6 (September 1953), 345–50.

Kemp, Friedhelm. "Renaissance du Poème," translated by Blaise Briod. *Cahiers de la Pléiade*, 9–10 (Summer-Autumn 1950), 133–35.

Richard, Jean-Pierre. "Saint-John Perse, Poète de la vivacité." *Cahiers du Sud*, 364–367 (December 1961–January 1962), 253–86.

Rougemont, Denis de. "Saint-John Perse et l'Amérique." *Cahiers de la Pléiade*, 9–10 (Summer-Autumn 1950), 136–39.

NOTE ON TRANSLATIONS

All translations from *Eloges and Other Poems*, *Exile and Other Poems*, *Seamarks*, *Winds*, *Chronique*, and *On Poetry* are from the bilingual editions listed above. All other translations are by the author.

Index

Frizeau, Gabriel, 9, 12; on Perse's malaise, 11
Future, 39, 41, 49, 76–79, 95–96

G
Genesis, 27; account of origin of universe in, 50
Gide, André, 63
God: as Creator, 5–6, 17, 28, 32–33, 50; poet as witness of, 17; as Holy Spirit, 57; immanent in universe, 57–58; purpose of, 58
Guadeloupe, 8; nostalgia of Perse for, 45
Guardian Angel, 56, 59–60

H
Human spirit: splendor of, 39–40
Humor, 101

I
"Images à Crusoé," 10, 18
Indian Ocean, 52
Infinite: essence of, 52
Intelligence, 72, 74–75; role and origin of, 5, 78
Intuition, 4, 16, 25, 34, 41, 42, 51, 63
"Invocation," 87, 92, 93

J
Jeune Fille Violaine, La, 10
Juxtaposition, 88–89, 95, 96, 99

K
Knowledge: role and origin of, 5

L
Laeta, 64
Language, 80–81; Perse's use of, 35, 81, 86; obscurity of, 81; resources of French, 83; Claudel's use of, 86; and theme, 86; organization of, 89; texture of, 101
Larbaud, Valéry, 82
Lectures sur la Botanique, 12
"Légende de Prakriti," 50, 71
Léger, Alexis Saint-Léger. *See* Perse, Saint-John
"Lettre à l'Abbé Brémond sur le vers français," 81

Life: transiency of, 65–66
Liturgy: *Miserere,* 67
Lorigiola, P., 24, 61
Louis d'Orléans, 8
Love: cosmic, 42, 44, 48–49, 75; role of, 42, 47, 59–60, 75; human, 44–47 *passim,* 59–62 *passim*; compared to sea, 45; and salvation, 59, 62; creative act of, 59, 62; divine as parallel to human, 59–62; and sacrifice, 61, 62, 75–76; power of, 66

M
"Magnificat," 16, 17, 24, 54, 56, 61, 62, 64, 65, 88
"Maison Fermée, La," 24, 51, 55, 56, 81, 99, 103
Mallarmé, Stéphane, 6, 15, 84
Man: role in universe, 5–6; will of, 39, 62–63; splendor of creation, 41, 71; void in, 41, 55–56, 60; cruelty of, 43; greed of, 43, 48; new race of, 44, 74; rehabilitation of, 48–49; exile and alienation of, 56, 60–61, 65, 74; personal unity of, 63, 75–76; obligation of, 71, 76, 78, 79; mastery of, over matter, 72–73, 78; passion for depravity of, 74; self-determination of, 76–78
Mankind: solidarity of, 22, 40, 55, 57, 60, 71–76 *passim,* 101; future of, 39, 42, 44, 76, 79
Mémoires Improvisés, 9, 88
"Mer de Baal, Mer de Mammon," 74, 88
Mésa, 53, 54, 59–62 *passim*
Messe là-bas, La, 56, 57, 58, 61, 63, 64, 66, 67
Metaphor, 6, 48, 88, 96, 98, 101
Micah: prophecy about war, 44
Milhaud, Darius: Claudel's comment on score for *Les Euménides,* 99–100
Mnemosyne, 96
Mondor, Henri: meaning of "Endormie," 10
Moreau, Pierre, 81

Scholars have long studied the moods, ideas, and techniques in the work of Paul Claudel and of Saint-John Perse, two of the leading French writers of this century. Each poet has created an epic vision of the universe through his concept of reality, his evaluation of the poet's function, and his nontraditional poetic form.

In many ways Claudel and Perse reveal a similarity in their purpose and design, yet there are striking differences in their outlook. Claudel's view is Christian in orientation and concerns itself with the human soul; his intuitions are focused on God. Perse is preoccupied with cosmic forces, especially the elements, space, time, duration, man's presence and history, and universal disorder. For Claudel, outer turbulence is equated with that which exists in man's soul; for Perse, the violent manifestations of the physical world are those of the history of man and his civilizations.

Though they seem to be ideological opposites, these major poets of an older generation both articulate an idealism that this generation values. Their work suggests that human solidarity will come about through universal love—for Claudel, it will be possible through a communion of souls, for Perse, through a communion of minds.

1972